2

Sequential Spelling

Teacher's Guide
Revised Edition

GW00685492

end
tend
intend
extend
attend
attend**ance**

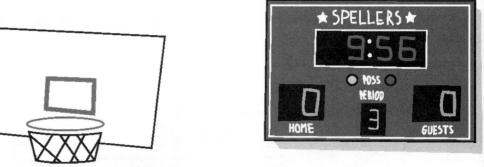

★ SPELLERS ★

9:56

POSS
PERIOD
3
HOME
GUESTS
0 0

COACH

Teacher's Guide
Revised Edition

1 Printing   Year 13

Publisher's Cataloging in Publication Data

Wave 3 Learning, Inc. *Sequential Spelling*.—Rev. ed., Arlington Heights, IL: *Wave 3 Learning*, Inc. c2013.
        Volume 2 of a 5 Volume series.

1. Spelling—Miscellanea. 2. Reading—Miscellanea. 3. Curriculum—Miscellanea 4. Literacy and Tutor Reference Tool.
Library of Congress Subject Headings: Spelling, Curriculum
Library of Congress Classification Number: LB1050.2F79
Library of Congress Card Number: To be determined
Dewey Decimal Classification Number 428.4
ISBN: 9781935943082

About *Sequential Spelling*

Sequential Spelling is a research-based system rooted in the classic Orton-Gillingham approach to learning. Developed almost forty years ago by a dyslexic to serve the needs of dyslexic students, it has since become the Gold Standard for spelling instruction for students who struggle for any reason...and a great many students who do not struggle at all!

Sequential Spelling teaches inductively, by doing, rather than using a rules-based approach. The simple reasons for this are two fold. First, realistically, the spelling of the English Language cannot be said to have a truly consistent set of rules. If you search on the internet for English Language spelling rules, you will get answers from six to over fifty rules. Each will have numerous exceptions and most are conceived in such a way that teaching them to a student of six to ten years of age is hopelessly optimistic. Most adults are unable to understand and apply them. What is a six-year-old to do? Second, inductive learning is hard-wired into the human brain. It is the same means by which your child learned to walk or to talk. It is the same means by which your student will learn everything of any importance in their life except mathematics and physical sciences...and note, both of those DO have hard and fast rules.

The curriculum provides multi-sensory spelling instruction. The student learns sets of words that share patterns of spelling rather than thematically related lists of words. This methodology enables the student with a learning difference to focus on learning a given sequence of letters, how they sound, and the words they appear in. The child who excels and move forward as quickly as they choose.

About this Edition

This edition of the *Sequential Spelling* series has been expanded. Each level now has a coordinating student workbook, complete with a daily "Using Your Words" activity. The teaching methodology described in the earlier edition has remained the same; however, the teacher guide now includes an answer key.

Wave 3 Learning
January 2013

Table of Contents

To the Teacher

<u>OVERVIEW</u>

Sequential Spelling uses word families or word patterns as its teaching method. The student learns the phonics sounds necessary for decoding words while learning to spell. For example, if you can teach the word **at** you can also teach:

bat	bats	batted	batting		
cat	cats				
scat	scats				
flat	flats	flatted	flatting		
pat	pats	patted	patting		
spat	spats				
mat	mats	matted	matting		
rat	rats	ratted	ratting		
batter	batters	battered	battering	battery	batteries
flatter	flatters	flattered	flattering	flattery	
matter	matters	mattered	mattering		
battle	battles	battled	battling		
cattle					
rattle	rattles	rattled	rattling		

similarly, from the word **act** you can build:

act	acts	acted	acting	active	action
fact	facts				
tract	tracts	traction			
attract	attracts	attracted	attracting	attractive	attraction
distract	distracts	distracted	distracting	distraction	
extract	extracts	extracted	extracting	extractive	extraction
subtract	subtracts	subtracted	subtracting	subtraction	
contract	contracts	contracted	contracting	contraction	

Spelling rules are not specifically taught in this curriculum. Rather, they are learned as part of the daily spelling lesson. A description of some of the more frequently used spelling rules is included at the end of this Guide.

<u>HALLMARKS OF *SEQUENTIAL SPELLING*</u>

- daily spelling tests with immediate feedback
- multi-sensory teaching (audio, visual, kinesthetic and oral) of spelling patterns
- base words are introduced first, then the endings for them (-s, -ed, -ing) on subsequent days.
- 180 lessons per level
- levels are not matched to grade level. Most students should begin at level 1.

Teaching the Lessons

MATERIALS NEEDED:

- Easel or dry erase board
- Different colored markers
- Student Workbook or notebook paper
- Teacher's guide

LESSON TIME:

15-20 minutes

LESSON PREPARATION:

Review the words for the spelling test before beginning the lesson to familiarize yourself with tricky spellings, homophones, etc.

Have students open their workbooks and find the page for the day's lesson. If they are using notebook paper for the spelling test, use one sheet per lesson.

LESSON FORMAT:

Each day will consist of a spelling test. Rather than teaching the spelling of each word, teachers should concentrate on teaching the basic sounds of each word. For example, when you are teaching the word family **–ange** (*range, ranges, arrange, arranges, arrangement, arrangements*) what is important is the teaching of the **–ange** ending, the plural ending and the **–ment** suffix as well as the initial consonant sounds and consonant blends.

Teaching Methodology
- Give each word separately.
- Say the word. Give it in a sentence. Repeat the word once more for clarity.
- Let the student(s) attempt the spelling.
- Give the correct spelling. Let each student correct their own spelling. Then give the next word.

Teaching Steps
Using contrasting marker colors will allow your students to more easily recognize the word patterns in each word. For example: when you give the correct spelling of **spinning** write the base **–in** in your base word color. Then, "*double the **n** and add **ing** to get **inning**.*" Add **p** and **s** in a contrasting color to get **spinning.**

NOTE: The most common mistake made in teaching *Sequential Spelling* is to give the entire test and then correct it. Students must self correct after each word, not at the end of the test.

Extra practice with homophone lists

At the bottom of each page are lists of homophones (words which sound exactly alike but have different meanings as well as spellings). You may want to include some practice of these concepts in your spelling lessons. Here are a few ideas for teaching homophones:

Homophone Pictionary – Give your student a card with the homophone pair and have them draw pictures of each. The other students can guess the homophones.

Silly Sentences – Give your students a list of homophone pairs and have them come up with silly sentences using the homophone pair.

Homophone Old Maid – Make about twenty pairs of cards with a homophone written on them. Include an "old maid" card as well. Deal the cards as evenly as possible. Then play "Old Maid." When there is a match, have the student show both cards and define EACH word in the homophone pair or use them correctly in a sentence.

ABC Homophone - Have your students come up with twenty-six homophone pairs, one for each letter of the alphabet.

Student Book

The student workbook (available separately from *Wave 3 Learning www.Wave3Learning.com*) has a "Using Your Words" section after each lesson. Students are given brief assignments to stretch their use of the words they have just learned. Four *Story Starter* pages are also included at the back of the book for use as creative writing exercises. The answer key for the student workbook is in this teacher edition. After teaching the day's lesson, you can choose to have your student complete the "Using Your Words" section of their workbook, extend the lesson as described below or move on to another subject.

PROGRESS EVALUATION

Evaluation tests are provided after the 40th, 80th, 120th, 160th and 180th lessons. If you choose to create other tests for grading purposes, they should be given at a separate time and students should be graded on their learning of the spelling of the sounds—not the words.

Administering the Evaluation Tests

Read the tests aloud to your students and ask them to complete the word in the sentence. Initial consonants and blends are given – only the spelling pattern used is tested. Note: If your students are not using the student workbook, you may download the student version of the levaluation tests in pdf format free of charge from the Wave 3 Learning website, *www.Wave3Learning.com*.

If you have any questions about how to teach the text, please do not hesitate to contact us at info@ wave3learning.com. We will respond same day to most questions.

ABOUT THE TEACHER TEXT

Notations

* asterisks remind the teacher that the word has a homophone (same pronunciation, different spelling) or heteronym (same spelling, different word and different pronunciation), or does not follow the normal pattern. For example, gyp ** should logically be spelled "jip." Similarly, the word proper ** should logically be spelled "propper" just like hopper, and copper, and stopper, but it is not. Homophones and homographs are listed for your convenience so that you make sure to use the word correctly in a sentence, like "billed. We were billed for extra carpeting. billed" or "build. We will build our house on a hill. build"

Abbreviations   Am = American spelling   Br = British spelling

Words in Bold Print

These are the most commonly used words and the most important to learn. Some words (like doesn't) don't follow regular word patterns and are repeated many times throughout the series. So, you do not have to use all the words in each word list, but please make sure you cover all the words in bold print. At the end of this curriculum, your students should be able to spell the most common words and have learned the most common patterns that occur in words.

Student Handwriting Expectations

Since the students correct their own spelling, they should be expected to write clearly and legibly. The daily tests can and should be used for handwriting practice because the patterns, being repetitive, can be a help in developing legible handwriting. As the teacher, you should set clear standards for acceptable handwriting on these spelling tests.

Customizing *Sequential Spelling* for your student

Change the Words on the Tests

You may decide you want to add, change or delete some words on each day's spelling list. Great! If you would prefer to start with a different word family, feel free. *Sequential Spelling* lists most of the words in each family, but not all. For the ambitious who would like to delve more deeply, we have a resource called Patterns of English Spelling which you may purchase from us by special order. *Please feel free to contact us at info@wave3learning.com*

Give the Test Again

If you decide to give the test again, allow at least two hours between re-tests. We also recommend that the absolute maximum number of times that *Sequential Spelling* tests be given each day is four times.

Increase/Decrease the Pace

Increase the time spent each day on spelling. You could try going through four days of *Sequential Spelling* 1 every day until it is finished and then move through four days of *Sequential Spelling* 2 every day, and continue on through four levels of *Sequential Spelling* in six months.

Lets get started!

Spelling Lists

	1st day	2nd day	3rd day	4th day
1.	* **chew**	* **chews**	chewed	chewing
2.	crew	* **crews**	I **knew** it.	We knew it.
3.	screw	screws	screwed	screwing
4.	brew	* **brews**	* **brewed**	brewing
5.	* **blew**	**drew**	withdrew	I * **threw** it.
6.	* **new**	news	newer	newest
7.	renew	renews	renewed	renewing
8.	strew	strews	strewed	strewing
9.	stew	stews	stewed	stewing
10.	dew	Jew	Jews	Jewish
11.	* **few**	fewer	fewest	pew
12.	* phew¹	whew	just a few	few
13.	**nephew**	nephews	nephews	nephew
14.	skew	skews	skewed	skewing
15.	spew	spews	spewed	spewing
16.	* aw	awe	**awful**	**awfully**
17.	**law**	laws	lawful	unlawful
18.	flaw	flaws	flawed	flaws
19.	claw	* **claws**	* **clawed**	clawing
20.	thaw	thaws	thawed	thawing
21.	**jaw**	jaws	jawed	jawing
22.	**draw**	draws	drawn	drawing
23.	straw	straws	drawer	drawers
24.	paw	* **paws**	pawed	pawing
25.	squaw	squaws	drew	drew

* Homophones:

chew/choo	You can chew gum when you are on a "choo-choo" train.
chews/choose	He chews bubble gum instead of tobacco. Let's choose up sides.
crews/cruise	We have four different work crews. I love my cruise control when I drive.
brews/bruise	A brewer brews beer in a brewery. How did you get that bruise on your arm?
brewed/brood	The cook brewed some coffee. You don't have to sit and brood all day.
new/knew/gnu	What's new? I thought you knew we just got our first gnu at the zoo.
through/threw	We are almost through. Who threw the ball?
blew/blue	The wind blew. The sky is blue.
few/phew	Win a few. Lose a few. Phew! That was close!
paws/pause	A cat walks on four paws. Let's pause here for a break?
claws/clause	We had our cat's claws removed. A clause is part of a sentence.
clawed/Claude	The cat clawed the curtains to shreds. Have you seen the paintings of Claude Monet?
aw/awe	Aw, don't feel too bad! We looked out over the valley from the mountaintop with a feeling of awe.

See the complete -ew family on p. 316 in *The Patterns of English Spelling* (TPES); the -aw, p. 319.

---

¹The word phew should be pronounced as half whistle, half sigh of relief. It falls into the same category as other words that lack a vowel sound, such as sh-h!, psst, and tsk.

	5th day	6th day	7th day	8th day
1.	**lawn**	lawns	awning	awnings
2.	pawn	pawns	pawned	pawning
3.	spawn	spawns	spawned	spawning
4.	**dawn**	dawns	dawned	dawning
5.	fawn	fawns	fawned	fawning
6.	yawn	yawns	yawned	yawning
7.	**talk**	talks	**talked**	talking
8.	stalk	stalks	stalked	stalking
9.	**walk**	walks	walked	**walking**
10.	sidewalk	sidewalks	walker	walkers
11.	balk	balks	balked	balking
12.	chalk	chalks	chalked	chalking
13.	* **calk**	calks	calked	calked
14.	* **caulk**	caulks	caulked	caulked
15.	milk	milks	milked	milking
16.	silk	silks	silky	silkiest
17.	bilk	bilks	bilked	bilking
18.	hawk	hawks	hawked	hawking
19.	Mohawk	Mohawks	**We're** going to win.	**They're** coming.
20.	gawk	gawks	gawked	gawking
21.	awkward	awkwardly	You're going to lose.	**He's** going.
22.	**sing**	sings	sang/sung	singing
23.	* **ring**[1]	rings	rang/rung	ringing
24.	* **wring**	wrings	wrung	wringing
25.	**spring**	springs	sprang/sprung	springing

* Homophones:

ring/wring   Put that ring on your finger or I'll wring your neck.

calk/caulk   You can calk around the windows or caulk around the windows. Your choice.

Note: The preferred spelling of /kawk/ is caulk.

See the complete -awn family on p. 423 in *The Patterns of English Spelling* (TPES); the -awk, p. 410; the -alk, p. 410; the -ilk, p. 245; -ing, p. 218.

---

[1]Although we conjugate the verb ring as ring, rang, rung, bring is conjugated as bring, brought, brought. Likewise, swing is conjugated swing, swung, swung.

                                              Sequential Spelling Level 2 - Teacher's Guide

	9th day	10th day	11th day	12th day
1.	cling	clings	clung	clinging
2.	fling	flings	flung	flinging
3.	sling	slings	slung	slinging
4.	**string**	strings	strung	stringing
5.	**bring**	brings	brought	bringing
6.	wing	**wings**	winged	winging
7.	swing	swings	swung	**swinging**
8.	ping	pings	pinged	pinging
9.	ding	dings	dinged	dinging
10.	sting	stings	stung	stinging
11.	thing	things	stinger	stingers
12.	anything	everything	**nothing**	nothing
13.	king	kings	**again**	again
14.	lung	lungs	**against**	against
15.	dung	gung ho	**any**	anybody
16.	tone	tones	toned	toning
17.	**stone**	stones	stoned	stoning
18.	**bone**	bones	boned	boning
19.	cone	cones	boner	bony
20.	* **lone**	lonely	* **alone**	lonesome
21.	clone	clones	cloned	cloning
22.	cyclone	cyclones	zone	zones
23.	**tune**	tunes	tuned	tuning
24.	attune	attunes	attuned	attuning
25.	immune	immunity	immunize	immunization

* Homophones:

loan/lone   The Lone Ranger couldn't get a loan.

a loan/alone He was all alone when he went for a loan.

See the complete -ing family on p. 218 in *The Patterns of English Spelling* (TPES); the -ung, p. 219; the -one, p. 339; the -une, p. 340.

	13th day	14th day	15th day	16th day
1.	prune	prunes	pruned	pruning
2.	dune	dunes	Neptune	Neptune's
3.	commune	comm**unity**	communities	communion
4.	opportune	**opportunity**	opportunities	opportunity
5.	bob	bobs	bobbed	bobbing
6.	sob	sobs	sobbed	sobbing
7.	cob	cobs	gob	gobs
8.	lob	lobs	lobbed	lobbing
9.	blob	blobs	lobby	lobbies
10.	slob	slobs	knob	knobs
11.	mob	mobs	mobbed	mobbing
12.	**rob**	robs	**robbed**	robbing
13.	robber	robbers	robbery	robberies
14.	throb	throbs	throbbed	throbbing
15.	**hope¹**	hopes	hoped	**hoping**
16.	dope	dopes	doped	doping
17.	lope	lopes	loped	loping
18.	mope	mopes	moped	moping
19.	elope	elopes	eloped	eloping
20.	slope	slopes	sloped	sloping
21.	**rope**	ropes	roped	roping
22.	grope	gropes	groped	groping
23.	cope	copes	coped	coping
24.	**scope**	scopes	scoped	scoping
25.	telescope	telescopes	microscope	microscopes

See the complete -une family on p. 340 in *The Patterns of English Spelling* (TPES); the -ob, p. 104; the -ope, p. 342.

¹*hoped* and *hoping* are often misspelled as *hopped* and *hopping* and vice versa.

	17th day	18th day	19th day	20th day
1.	**back**	backs	backed	backing
2.	hack	hacks	hacked	hacking
3.	jack	jacks	jacked	jacking
4.	hijack	hijacks	hijacked	hijacking
5.	hacker	hackers	hijacker	hijackers
6.	lack	* lacks	lacked	**lacking**
7.	**black**	blacks	blacker	blackest
8.	slack	slacks	slacked	slacking
9.	clack	clacks	clacked	clacking
10.	snack	snacks	snacked	snacking
11.	**pack**	**packs**	* **packed**	**packing**
12.	unpack	unpacks	unpacked	unpacking
13.	repack	repacks	repacked	repacking
14.	tack	* **tacks**	* **tacked**	tacking
15.	stack	stacks	stacked	stacking
16.	rack	racks	racked	racking
17.	**track**	**tracks**	* **tracked**	tracking
18.	crack	cracks	**cracked**	cracking
19.	attack	attacks	**attacked**	attacking
20.	**stack**	stacks	stacked	stacking
21.	shack	shacks	**cracker**	**crackers**
22.	smack	smacks	smacked	smacking
23.	quack	quacks	quacked	quacking
24.	**sack**	* **sacks**	sacked	sacking
25.	whack	whacks	whacked	whacking

* Homophones:

lacks/lax	He lacks discipline. She is lax about enforcing rules.
tacks/tax	Is there a tax on thumb tacks?
packed/pact	They packed a whole lot of items in their pact for peace.
tacked/tact	He didn't show any tact when he tacked his poster over his opponent's.
tracked/tract	We tracked the animals on a lonely tract of land.
sacks/sax	We bought two sacks of groceries and a new sax.

See the complete -act family on p. 223 in *The Patterns of English Spelling* (TPES).

	21st day	22nd day	23rd day	24th day
1.	**check**	checks	checked	**checking**
2.	deck	decks	decked	decking
3.	**neck**	necks	checker	**checkers**
4.	peck	pecks	pecked	pecking
5.	heck	reckless	recklessly	wrecker
6.	wreck	**wrecks**	**wrecked**	wrecking
7.	fleck	flecks	flecked	flecking
8.	**sick**	sickly	sickest	sickness
9.	**lick**	licks	**licked**	licking
10.	slick	slicks	slicked	slicking
11.	flick	flicks	flicked	flicking
12.	flicker	flickers	flickered	flickering
13.	**click**	clicks	**clicked**	clicking
14.	**kick**	kicks	kicked	kicking
15.	nick	**nicks**	nicked	nicking
16.	knickknack	knickers	kicker	kickers
17.	**pick**	**picks**	picked	picking
18.	prick	pricks	clicker	clickers
19.	**trick**	**tricks**	tricked	tricking
20.	brick	bricks	bricked	bricking
21.	tick	ticks	ticked	ticking
22.	**stick**	sticks	stuck	sticking
23.	wick	wicks	chick	chicks
24.	**quick**	quicker	quickest	quickly
25.	chick	chicks	**chicken**	chickens

See the complete -eck family on p. 215 in *The Patterns of English Spelling* (TPES); the –ick p. 215.

	25th day	26th day	27th day	28th day
1.	* **ax**	axes	axed	axing
2.	**ask**	**asks**	**asked**	**asking**
3.	* **axe**	climax	flax	Max
4.	* **lax**	* **sax**	saxophone	saxophones
5.	relax	relaxes	relaxed	relaxing
6.	**wax**	waxes	**waxed**	waxing
7.	**six**	sixes	sixty	sixteen
8.	**mix**	**mixes**	**mixed**	**mixing**
9.	**fix**	fixes	**fixed**	**fixing**
10.	prefix	prefixes	sixth	* **nix**
11.	suffix	suffixes	pixie	pixies
12.	mixer	mixers	mixture	mixtures
13.	remix	remixes	fixture	fixtures
14.	* **coax**	coaxes	coaxed	coaxing
15.	hoax	hoaxes	hoaxed	hoaxing
16.	**box**	boxes	**boxed**	**boxing**
17.	fox	foxes	foxed	foxing
18.	outfox	outfoxes	outfoxed	outfoxing
19.	* **sox**	* **lox**	Mr. Cox	pox
20.	ox	oxen	* **phlox**	smallpox
21.	**fast**	fasts	fasted	fasting
22.	breakfast	* **mast**	masts	in the * **past**
23.	cast	casts	casters	casting
24.	broadcast	broadcasts	broadcasted	broadcasting
25.	**last**	lasts	lasted	lasting

* Homophones:

ax/axe	A lumberjack uses an ax (axe).
sax/sacks	Tom plays the sax. His brother plays with sacks and boxes.
lax/lacks	Lax law enforcement lacks the ability to control.
coax/cokes	We used to coax our folks for extra cokes.
sox/socks	He bought a pair of sox. She bought a pair of socks.
past/passed	In the past, students were passed despite their failing grades.
mast/massed	The sailors massed around the mast.
lox/locks/loughs	You can eat lox, use locks, and swim in Irish loughs.
phlox/flocks	Shepherds herd flocks of sheep. Phlox are flowers.

See the complete -ax family on p. 265 in *The Patterns of English Spelling* (TPES); the -ix, p. 267; the -ox, p. 268; the -oax, p. 268; -ast, p. 233.

	29th day	30th day	31st day	32nd day
1.	blast	blasts	blasted	blasting
2.	vast	vastly	yeast	anymore
3.	**east**	eastern	northeast wind	easterly
4.	Easter	Easterner	the Northeast	the Southeast
5.	feast	feasts	feasted	feasting
6.	**beast**	beasts	**at least**	southeast wind
7.	**Christ**	Christ's	**Christmas¹**	Xmas
8.	**Christian**	Christians	persistent	existence
9.	**Christianity**	consistent	consistently	persistently
10.	**list**	lists	listed	listing
11.	enlist	enlists	enlisted	enlisting
12.	**assist**	assists	assisted	assisting
13.	insist	insists	**insisted**	insisting
14.	consist	consists	consisted	consisting
15.	persist	persists	persisted	persisting
16.	resist	resists	resisted	resisting
17.	*** mist**	mists	misted	misting
18.	**twist**	twists	twisted	twisting
19.	whist	assistant	*** assistants**	*** assistance**
20.	grist	insistent	persistent	resistance
21.	**exist**	exists	existed	existing
22.	**boast**	boasts	boasted	boasting
23.	**coast**	coasts	coasted	coaster
24.	**roast**	roasts	roaster	roasting
25.	**toast**	toasted	toasting	toaster

* Homophones:

assistants/assistance   The two assistants gave the doctor assistance.

mist/missed   We missed the heavy mist of London.

See the complete -ast family on p. 233 in *The Patterns of English Spelling* (TPES); the -east, p. 237; the -ist, p. 235; the -oast, p. 235.

¹The X in Christmas comes from the Greek letter X that the word Christ in Greek begins with.

	33rd day	**34th day**	**35th day**	**36th day**
1.	**lost**	lost	lost	lost
2.	**cost**	costs	costly	frosty
3.	accost	accosts	accosted	accosting
4.	**frost**	frosts	frosted	frosting
5.	defrost	defrosts	defrosted	defrosting
6.	*** must**	musty	*** mustard**	custard
7.	dust	dusts	dusted	dusting
8.	just	justly	dusty	duster
9.	adjust	adjusts	adjusted	adjusting
10.	readjust	readjusts	readjusted	readjusting
11.	gust	gusts	gusted	gusting
12.	disgust	disgusts	**disgusted**	disgusting
13.	rust	rusts	rusted	rusting
14.	crust	crusts	crusty	trusty
15.	*** trust**	trusts	trusted	trusting
16.	thrust	thrusts	thrust	thrusting
17.	*** bust**	busts	busted	busting
18.	robust	burst	bursts	bursting
19.	beam	beams	beamed	beaming
20.	ream	reams	reamed	reaming
21.	**cream**	creams	creamed	creaming
22.	**scream**	screams	screamed	screaming
23.	**dream**	dreams	dreamed	dreaming
24.	**stream**	streams	streamed	streaming
25.	**steam**	steams	steamed	steaming

* Homophones:

must/mussed	He must go. He mussed up his hair.
trust/trussed	We trust you. Make sure he is trussed up tightly.
bust/bussed	The police made a bust. The children were bussed to school.
mustard/mustered	I like catsup and mustard. He was mustered out of the army.

See the complete -ost family on p. 235 in *The Patterns of English Spelling* (TPES); the -ust, p. 236; the -eam, p. 418.

	37th day	38th day	39th day	40th day
1.	* team	teams	teamed	* teaming
2.	steam	steams	steamed	steaming
3.	* seam	seams	seamstress	seamstresses
4.	gleam	gleams	gleamed	gleaming
5.	squeamish	creamer	creamery	dreamers
6.	streamer	streamers	steamer	screamer
7.	lame	came	became	overcame
8.	blame	blames	blamed	blaming
9.	flame	flames	flamed	flaming
10.	fame	fame	famous	famously
11.	game	games	endgame	ashamed of
12.	name	names	named	naming
13.	nickname	nicknames	nicknamed	nicknaming
14.	surname	surnames	tame	tamely
15.	shame	shames	shamed	shaming
16.	dame	dames	ashamed	ashamed
17.	frame	frames	framed	framing
18.	hem	hems	hemmed	hemming
19.	emblem	emblems	mayhem	harem
20.	them	gem	themselves	them
21.	stem	stems	stemmed	stemming
22.	gem	gems	long-stemmed	condemnation
23.	condemn[1]	condemns	condemned	condemning
24.	from	from	from	from
25.	mom	prom	bomb[1]	bombs

* Homophones:

seam/seem It would seem that this seam is about to split.

teaming/teeming They were teaming up against us. The pond was teeming with fish.

bomb/balm Applying balm to itchy or chapped skin is soothing. A bomb isn't.

See the complete -eam family on p. 418 in *The Patterns of English Spelling* (TPES); the -ame, p. 332; the -em, p. 117; the -om, p. 119.

[1] There is a silent n at the end of condemn and a silent b at the end of bomb. See section on silent letters in *The Patterns of English Spelling*, pp. 958-961.

Sequential Spelling Level 2 - Teacher's Guide

Evaluation Test #1 (After 40 Days)

		Pattern being tested	Lesson word is in
1.	Not all Irishmen love an Irish s**tew.**	ew	1
2.	I have all kinds of nieces and neph**ews.**	ews	2
3.	I wouldn't want to live in a house made of str**aw.**	aw	1
4.	It's awfully sloppy when it's th**awing** outside.	awing	4
5.	It d**awned** on me that today's the day for a test.	awned	7
6.	The Moh**awks** are a proud tribe of American Indians.	awks	6
7.	They're always s**inging** songs.	inging	8
8.	Rolling st**ones** gather no moss.	ones	10
9.	Musicians are good at t**uning** their instruments.	uning	12
10.	They keep complaining that they were r**obbed.**	obbed	15
11.	We were h**oping** that they would grow up.	oping	16
12.	The auditorium was just jam-p**acked** with people.	acked	19
13.	I enjoy a good game of ch**eckers** once in a while.	eckers	24
14.	You shouldn't have k**icked** him in the shins.	icked	23
15.	I **asked** him to please behave.	asked	27
16.	Perry Como is always very rel**axed.**	axed	27
17.	The program l**asted** for only twenty minutes.	asted	27
18.	I thought it would last for at l**east** thirty.	east	31
19.	We bought them a t**oaster** for their wedding present.	oaster	32
20.	We were disg**usted** with their selfish behavior.	usted	35

	41st day	42nd day	43rd day	44th day
1.	**faith**	faithful	faithfully	faithfulness
2.	**math**	unfaithful	unfaithfully	unfaithfulness
3.	**bath**	baths	path	paths
4.	bathe	bathes	bathed	bathing
5.	**path**	paths	warpath	warpaths
6.	aftermath	lath	wrath	towpath
7.	**father**	fathers	fathered	fathering
8.	**mother**	mothers	mothered	mothering
9.	smother	smothers	smothered	smothering
10.	**brother**	brothers	stepbrother	stepfather
11.	bother	bothers	bothered	bothering
12.	**south**	in the South	**with**	**without**
13.	mouth	mouths	**anyplace**	**anything**
14.	method	methods	**aren't**	**hadn't**
15.	**death**	deaths	**my * aunt**	**my * aunts**
16.	breath	breaths	*** Aunt** Mary	my * **aunt's** hat
17.	**breathe**	breathes	breathed	breathing
18.	**cloth**	cloths	because	because
19.	clothe	*** clothes**	clothed	clothing
20.	**health**	healthy	healthier	healthiest
21.	**wealth**	wealthy	wealthier	wealthiest
22.	bum	bums	bummed	bumming
23.	*** sum**	sums	summed	summing
24.	**gum**	gums	summary	summaries
25.	hum	hums	hummed	humming

* Homophones:

clothes/close	I love to buy new clothes. Please close the door,.
sum/some	He won a large sum of money. I would like some of his luck.
ant/aunt/Aunt Mary	My Aunt Mary was bitten by a fire ant. Is your aunt coming to the party?
ants/aunts/aunt's	She used her aunt's collection of ants as a science project.

See the complete -aith family on p. 278 in *The Patterns of English Spelling* (TPES); the -ath, p. 275; the -eath, p. 275; the -eathe, p. 279; -oth, p. 218; -othe, 279; -athe, p. 279; -ealth, p. 280; -um, p. 120.

	45th day	46th day	47th day	48th day
1.	**drum**	drums	drummed	drumming
2.	chum	chums	chummed	chumming
3.	* **plum**	plums	drummer	drummers
4.	* **plumb**	plumbs	plumbed	plumbing
5.	**crumb**	**crumbs**	plumber	plumbers
6.	**thumb**	**thumbs**	thumbed	thumbing
7.	**dumb**	dumber	dumbest	dumb
8.	slum	slums	slummed	slumming
9.	glum	mum	mums	**I'd**
10.	scum	yum	* **clothes**	* **clothes**
11.	autumn	autumns	**aren't**	aren't
12.	column	columns	**hadn't**	**doesn't**
13.	* **son**	sons	bacon	dragon
14.	ton	tons	* **won**	wagon
15.	**common**	commonly	uncommon	uncommonly
16.	**gallon**	gallons	sermon	sermons
17.	bun	buns	bunny	bunnies
18.	gun	guns	gunned	gunning
19.	**fun**	**funny**	funnier	funniest
20.	stun	stuns	stunned	**stunning**
21.	**shun**[1]	**shuns**	**shunned**	**shunning**
22.	* **sun**	suns	sunned	sunning
23.	**run**	runs	**ran**	**running**
24.	* **nun**	nuns	runner	**runners**
25.	* **none**	**no one**	**none**	**none**

* Homophones:

plum/plumb	He ate an apple, a pear, and a plum. She knows how to use a plumb bob.
close/clothes	Please close the clothes closet door.
sun/son	The sun is up. Their son is still in bed.
nun/none	The nun won none of the money.
one/won	Who was the one who won the money?

See the complete -um family on p. 120 in *The Patterns of English Spelling* (TPES); the -umb, p. 120; the -on, pp. 124, 835-851; the -un, p. 125.

[1]These are the only words in which the sound /shun/ is spelled shun. All other times the sound /shun/ is spelled one of three ways: tion as in nation; ssion as in mission; cion as in suspicion.

	49th day	50th day	51st day	52nd day
1.	pardon	pardons	pardoned	pardoning
2.	London	lesson	lessons	**aren't**
3.	poison	poisons	poisoned	poisoning
4.	weapon	weapons	*** clothes**	*** clothes**
5.	**iron**	irons	ironed	ironing
6.	**reason**	reasons	reasoned	reasoning
7.	treason	because	**I'd**	**because**
8.	**season**	seasons	seasoned	seasoning
9.	arson	many	**many**	**many**
10.	parson	parsons	**says**	**says**
11.	**prison**	prisons	prisoner	prisoners
12.	**ton**	tons	*** I'll**	*** I'll**
13.	carton	cartons	island	*** isle**
14.	melon	melons	felon	felons
15.	pun	puns	punned	punning
16.	spun	Hun	Huns	**island**
17.	* dun	duns	dunned	dunning
18.	*** done**	all done	well done	poorly **done**
19.	**sir**	sirs	*** fir**	**firs**
20.	**stir**	stirs	**stirred**	**stirring**
21.	whir	whirs	whirred	whirring
22.	**her**	hers	**herself**	*** were**
23.	refer	refers	**referred**	**referring**
24.	**prefer**	prefers	**preferred**	preferring
25.	**offer**	offers	offered	**offering**

---

* Homophones:

clothes/close   We need some new clothes. What time does the store close?

I'll/isle/aisle   I'll need a boat to go to that isle. Have you been down the aisle?

I'd/eyed   I'd take another look at that math problem. He eyed Jack's skateboard with interest.

fir/fur   You don't get fur from a fir tree.

done/dun   Are you done? The bank started to dun him for the money.

were/we're   Where were you? We're going to win.

See the complete -on family on pp. 835-851 in *The Patterns of English Spelling* (TPES); the -un, p. 125; the -ir, p. 514; the -er, p. 511.

	53rd day	54th day	55th day	56th day
1.	differ	differs	differed	differing
2.	**different**	differently	difference	differences
3.	suffer	suffers	suffered	**suffering**
4.	confer	confers	conferred	conferring
5.	*** infer**	infers	inferred	inferring
6.	transfer	transfers	transferred	transferring
7.	**cool**	cools	cooled	cooling
8.	fool	fools	fooled	**fooling**
9.	pool	pools	pooled	pooling
10.	spool	spools	spooled	spooling
11.	tool	**tools**	tooled	tooling
12.	drool	drools	drooled	drooling
13.	**school**	schools	schooled	schooling
14.	high school	grade school	unschooled	school age
15.	cab	cabs	lab	labs
16.	scab	scabs	slab	slabs
17.	blab	blabs	blabbed	blabbing
18.	flab	flabby	flabbier	flabbiest
19.	tab	tabs	tabbed	tabbing
20.	stab	stabs	stabbed	stabbing
21.	gab	gabs	gabbed	gabbing
22.	**grab**	grabs	grabbed	grabbing
23.	crab	crabs	grabby	grabbiest
24.	drab	drabs	**crabby**	crabbiest
25.	dab	dabs	dabbed	dabbing

*Homophones:

infer/in fur   I hope you didn't infer that I was angry at you. Many celebrities like to dress in fur.

See the complete -er family on p. 511 in *The Patterns of English Spelling* (TPES); the -ool, p. 414; the -ab, p. 101.

	57th day	58th day	59th day	60th day
1.	**food**	foods	* I'll	* **were**
2.	* **mood**	moods	moody	moodiest
3.	brood	broods	brooded	brooding
4.	fib	fibs	fibbed	fibbing
5.	bib	bibs	island	what
6.	rib	ribs	ribbed	ribbing
7.	crib	cribs	cribbed	cribbing
8.	lib	glib	squib	cribbage
9.	tub	tubs	rubber	rubbery
10.	stub	stubs	stubbed	stubbing
11.	dub	dubs	dubbed	dubbing
12.	cub	cubs	bub	chub
13.	nub	nubs	hubbub	chubby
14.	snub	snubs	snubbed	snubbing
15.	club	clubs	clubbed	clubbing
16.	flub	flubs	flubbed	flubbing
17.	rub	rubs	rubbed	rubbing
18.	scrub	scrubs	scrubbed	scrubbing
19.	drub	drubs	drubbed	drubbing
20.	grub	grubs	grubbed	grubbing
21.	shrub	shrubs	shrubbery	blubber
22.	sub	subs	subbed	subbing
23.	* **tea**	* **teas**	* **isle**	* **we're**
24.	* **pea**	* peas	* **sea**	* **seas**
25.	* **flea**	* fleas	plea	* **pleas**

* Homophones:

I'll/aisle/isle	**I'll** not go down any aisle on that isle.
we're/were	We're not interested in knowing where you were.
mood/mooed	I'm not in the mood to hear how the cow mooed.
tea/tee/	Drink your tea. In golf, you use a tee.
pleas/please	When she entered her client's pleas of not guilty, she said please.
sea/see/	If you can see the sea, say, "Si!"
seas/sees/seize	Oceans are bigger than seas. If he sees you, seize the moment.
tease/tees/teas	Don't tease me because I break so many golf tees or drink different teas.
were/we're	If you were paying attention, you'd know where we're going.
flea/flee	The bug spray made the flea flee.
pea/pee; peas/pees	A pea is a vegetable. "Pee" is a "taboo" word for urine or urinate.

See the complete -ood family on p. 404 in *The Patterns of English Spelling* (TPES); the -ib, p. 103; the -ub, p. 105; the -ea, p. 305.

Sequential Spelling Level 2 - Teacher's Guide

	61st day	62nd day	63rd day	64th day
1.	* peace	peaceful	peacefully	peaceful
2.	* piece	pieces	pieced	piecing
3.	niece	nieces	piecework	piecemeal
4.	head	heads	headed	heading
5.	forehead	foreheads	deadhead	deadheads
6.	* (**) read	redhead	blackhead	blackheads
7.	tread	treads	trod	treading
8.	treadle	treadles	downtrodden	aren't
9.	spread	spreads	spread	spreading
10.	* bread	breads	breaded	breading
11.	dread	dreads	dreaded	dreading
12.	stead	bedstead	dreadful	dreadfully
13.	steady	steadier	steadiest	steadily
14.	* (**) lead	pencil leads	instead	doesn't
15.	thread	threads	threaded	threading
16.	voice	voices	voiced	voicing
17.	invoice	invoices	invoiced	invoicing
18.	choice	choices	choicer	choicest
19.	rejoice	rejoices	rejoiced	rejoicing
20.	void	voids	voided	voiding
21.	* avoid	avoids	avoided	avoiding
22.	asteroid	asteroids	devoid	celluloid
23.	oil	oils	oiled	oiling
24.	boil	boils	boiled	boiling
25.	broil	broils	broiled	broiling

* Homophones:

peace/piece	I can't rest in peace until I give them a piece of my mind.
read/red	Have you read *The Red Badge of Courage?*
lead/led	The trail of the lead pencil led to his arrest.
bread/bred	The love of baking bread is bred into bakers.
avoid/a void	What means to stay away from nothing? Avoid a void!

** Heteronyms:

read/read	Read me a book that you haven't already read to me.
lead/lead	Lead me on, MacDuff. Show me how to make gold from lead.

See the complete -iece family on p. 432 in *The Patterns of English Spelling* (TPES); the -eace, p. 432; the -ead, p. 402; the -oice, p. 433; -oid, p. 403; -oil, 415.

	65th day	66th day	67th day	68th day
1.	foil	foils	foiled	foiling
2.	spoil	spoils	spoiled	spoiling
3.	toil	toils	toiled	toiling
4.	coil	coils	coiled	coiling
5.	recoil	recoils	recoiled	recoiling
6.	soil	soils	soiled	soiling
7.	turmoil	toilet	toilets	toiletry
8.	**join**	joins	joined	joining
9.	joint	joints	*** clothes**	**aren't**
10.	rejoin	rejoins	rejoined	rejoining
11.	coin	coins	coined	coining
12.	loin	loins	sirloin	sirloins
13.	tenderloin	tenderloins	groin	joiner
14.	**point**	points	pointed	pointing
15.	**appoint**	appoints	appointed	appointing
16.	disappoint	disappoints	**disappointed**	disappointing
17.	anoint	anoint	anointed	anointing
18.	ointment	appointment	disappointment	*** I'll**
19.	**loud**	loudly	louder	loudest
20.	*** aloud**	proud	proudly	proudest
21.	**cloud**	clouds	clouded	clouding
22.	cloudy	cloudier	cloudiest	thundercloud
23.	shroud	shrouds	shrouded	shrouding
24.	crowd	crowds	crowded	crowding
25.	*** you**	*** you're** it	*** your** house	**says**

* Homophones:

aloud/allowed	Anyone with a loud voice should be allowed to read aloud.
clothes/close	Please close the clothes closet door.
I'll/isle/aisle	I'll go down an aisle (in a store) on a misty isle (island).
you/ewe/yew	You should see a ewe make a U-turn around a yew.
your/you're	You're wanted at home. Your mother's calling.

See the complete -oil family on p. 415 in *The Patterns of English Spelling* (TPES); the -oin, p. 423; the -oint, p. 253; the -oud, p. 403; -owd, p. 403.

	69th day	70th day	71st day	72nd day
1.	**mouse**	**mice**	**I'd**	**because**
2.	louse	lice	**many**	**many**
3.	blouse	blouses	bloused	blousing
4.	douse	douses	doused	dousing
5.	** **house**	(n.) * **houses**	**because**	* **isle**
6.	to ** **house**	(v.) * **houses**	housed	**housing**
7.	spouse	spouses	playhouse	guardhouse
8.	youth	youthful	youthfulness	youths
9.	**save**	saves	saved	**saving**
10.	pave	paves	paved	paving
11.	**shave**	shaves	shaved	**shaving**
12.	rave	raves	raved	raving
13.	grave	graves	lifesaver	shaver
14.	engrave	engraves	engraved	engraving
15.	**brave**	braves	braved	braving
16.	braver	bravery	bravest	**bravely**
17.	**cave**	caves	caved	caving
18.	crave	craves	craved	craving
19.	**slave**	slaves	slaved	slaving
20.	slaver	slavery	**gave**	**forgave**
21.	* **wave**	waves	waved	waving
22.	* **waive**	waives	waived	waiving
23.	behave	behaves	behaved	behaving
24.	misbehave	misbehaves	misbehaved	misbehaving
25.	**have**	**haven't**	**having**	**haven't**

* Homophones:

wave/waive   Be careful or you'll waive your right to wave good-bye.

I'll/isle/aisle   I'll visit an isle, but I won't walk down the aisle.

houses/houses   A prison houses criminals in cells not houses.

** Heteronyms:

house ("HOW-zz")/house ("HOW-ss")   You don't have to house a criminal in his own house.

See the complete -ouse family on p. 433 in *The Patterns of English Spelling* (TPES); the -ave, p. 324.

27

	73rd day	74th day	75th day	76th day
1.	**safe**	safes	safety	safeties
2.	chafe	chafes	chafed	chafing
3.	strafe	strafes	strafed	strafing
4.	ravel	ravels	ravelled	ravelling
5.	unravel	unravels	raveled	raveling
6.	**travel**	**travels**	**traveled**	**traveling**
7.	**(Am.) traveler**	**travelers**	**travelled**	**travelling**
8.	**(Br.) traveller**[1]	**travellers**	gavelled	gavelling
9.	gavel	gavels	gaveled	gaveling
10.	life	nine lives	lifelike	my life's work
11.	**wife**	wives	fife	fifes
12.	rife	I have	I've	I've
13.	strife	**two knives**	you've	*** we've**
14.	**knife**	**knifes**	knifed	knifing
15.	(v.) ** **live**	** **lives**	lived	**living**
16.	relive	relives	relived	reliving
17.	olive	olives	liver	livers
18.	**give**	gives	gave	**giving**
19.	(adj.) ** live	lively	alive	lively
20.	dive	dives	dived	diving
21.	drive	drives	drove	**driving**
22.	**five**	fives	diver	driver
23.	arrive	arrives	arrived	**arriving**
24.	revive	revives	revived	reviving
25.	survive	survives	survived	surviving

* Homophones:

we've/weave   We've learned how to weave.

** Heteronyms:

live ("liv")/live ("LYH'v")   I live to listen to live music.

lives("livz")/lives("LYH'vz")   He lives alone and watches the TV show "Days of Our Lives."

See the complete -afe family on p. 324 in *The Patterns of English Spelling* (TPES); the -ive, p. 325; the -ife, p. 325; the -ave, p. 324.

[1]The preferred American spelling has the single *l* in words such as *traveled*. British spelling always uses the double l as in *travelled*.

Sequential Spelling Level 2 - Teacher's Guide

	77th day	78th day	79th day	80th day
1.	thrive	thrives	thrived	thriving
2.	deprive	deprives	deprived	depriving
3.	strive	strives	strived	striving
4.	**move**	moves	moved	**moving**
5.	remove	removes	removed	removing
6.	**prove**	proves	proved	**proving**
7.	approve	approves	**approved**	approving
8.	disapprove	disapproves	disapproved	disapproving
9.	**improve**	improves	improved	**improving**
10.	**movie**	movies	approval	improvement
11.	**am**	**I'm** going to go.[1]	* **You're** going to go.	* **We're** going to go.
12.	ram	rams	rammed	ramming
13.	cram	crams	crammed	cramming
14.	scram	scrams	scrammed	scramming
15.	dram	drams	gram	grams
16.	pram	prams	tram	trams
17.	jam	jams	jammed	jamming
18.	bam	Sam-I-Am	cam	cams
19.	* **dam**	dams	dammed	damming
20.	* **damn**[2]	damns	damned	damning
21.	ham	hams	hammed	hamming
22.	* **lam**	tam	sham	shams
23.	* **lamb**	lambs	wham	swam
24.	slam	slams	slammed	slamming
25.	clam	clams	clammed	clamming

* Homophones:

dam/damn	Never damn a dam. Dam a river instead.
lam/lamb	A man on the lam hasn't time to cook and eat lamb chops.
you're/your	You're going to get your answer soon enough.
We're/were	We're going to find out where you were.

See the complete -am family on p. 116 in *The Patterns of English Spelling* (TPES); the -ove, p. 326; the -ive, p. 325.

---

[1]Please read the words *going to* as "gonna"! This "Scrunching up" in speech, common to all dialects, is a phenomenon known to linguists as *synaloepha* or *sandhi*.

[2]*damn* is really short for *to condemn*. The **n** is silent in the short form but you hear it in the longer forms, dam**n**ation and condem**n**ation.

Evaluation Test #2 (After 80 Days)

		Pattern being tested	Lesson word is in
1.	The injured man scr**eamed** for help.	eamed	35
2.	You should be ash**amed** of yourself.	amed	39
3.	His f**ather** was a farmer.	ather	41
4.	Do you like liver sm**othered** in onions?	othered	43
5.	I would rather be h**ealthy** than to be sick.	ealthy	42
6.	I would rather hear him h**umming** than singing.	umming	44
7.	The whole team gave the th**umbs** up sign.	umbs	46
8.	The dress she wore to the awards show was st**unning.**	unning	48
9.	We donate our old cl**othes** to Goodwill.	othes	52
10.	Do you know who st**irred** up all that trouble?	irred	51
11.	I don't pay any attention to cr**abby** people.	abby	55
12.	The doctor scr**ubbed** her hands before operating.	ubbed	59
13.	The sleeping child looked very p**eace**ful.	eace	62
14.	Why don't we just watch TV inst**ead?**	ead	63
15.	The cook specialized in b**oiling** water.	oiling	64
16.	I hope you're not disapp**ointed** in me.	ointed	67
17.	I hate people who are always cr**owding** me.	owding	68
18.	She bought two new bl**ouses** at Macy's.	ouses	70
19.	That kid is always misbeh**aving**.	aving	72
20.	Did you see anything new on your tr**avels**?	avels	74

Sequential Spelling Level 2 - Teacher's Guide

	81st day	82nd day	83rd day	84th day
1.	*** him**	himself	*** him**	himself
2.	*** hymn**	hymns	hymnal	hymnal
3.	slim	slims	slimmed	slimming
4.	rim	rims	rimmed	rimming
5.	trim	trims	trimmed	trimming
6.	brim	brims	brimmed	brimming
7.	grim	prim	trimmer	trimmest
8.	dim	dims	dimmed	dimming
9.	**swim**	swims	swam/swum	**swimming**
10.	Tim	Tim's	Timothy	Timothy's
11.	victim	victims	*** Jim**	*** Jim's**
12.	whim	whims	*** gym**	*** gyms**
13.	shim	shims	shimmed	shimming
14.	skim	skims	skimmed	skimming
15.	Kim	Kim's whim	limb	limbs
16.	amp	amps	**camper**	campers
17.	**camp**	camps	camped	camping
18.	**champ**	champs	champion	champions
19.	lamp	lamps	championship	championships
20.	clamp	clamps	clamped	clamping
21.	tamp	tamps	tamped	tamping
22.	**stamp**	**stamps**	stamped	stamping
23.	ramp	ramps	scamp	scamps
24.	tramp	tramps	tramped	tramping
25.	cramp	**cramps**	cramped	cramping

* Homophones:

him/hymn   Please don't let him sing a hymn.

Jim/gym   Jim loves to play in a gym.

Jim's/gyms   He owns and operates several of Jim's gyms.

See the complete -im family on p. 118 in *The Patterns of English Spelling* TPES; the -amp, p. 269; the -ion, p. 843.

	85th day	86th day	87th day	88th day
1.	damp	damper	dampers	dampest
2.	dampen	dampens	dampened	dampening
3.	* **week**	weeks	weekend	weekends
4.	* **peek**	**peeks**	**peeked**	**peeking**
5.	reek	reeks	reeked	reeking
6.	creek	creeks	* **leek**	* **leeks**
7.	cheek	cheeks	sleek	meek
8.	seek	seeks	sought	seeking
9.	shriek	shrieks	shrieked	shrieking
10.	* **weak**	weaker	weakest	* **weakly**
11.	weaken	weakens	weakened	weakening
12.	beak	beaks	beaker	beakers
13.	* **peak**	**peaks**	sneaker	sneakers
14.	speak	speaks	spoke/spoken	speaking
15.	streak	streaks	streaked	streaking
16.	sneak	sneaks	sneaked	sneaking
17.	* **creak**	**creaks**	creaked	creaking
18.	squeak	squeaks	squeaked	squeaking
19.	freak	freaks	freaked	freaking
20.	* **leak**	**leaks**	leaked	leaking
21.	teak	speaker	speakers	squeaky
22.	**sleep**	sleeps	**slept**	sleeping
23.	oversleep	oversleeps	overslept	oversleeping
24.	**asleep**	sleeper	sleepers	* **clothes**
25.	**keep**	keeps	**kept**	keeping

* Homophones:

week/weak	All week I felt weak.
peek/peak/pique	A peek at Pike's Peak might pique your curiosity.
creek/creak	Creek rhymes with either seek or sick. Creak rhymes with reek.
weekly/weakly	The weekly paper is very weakly supported.
leek/leak	A leek is vegetable. A leak can sink a ship.
clothes/close	They had to close the used clothes store.

See the complete -amp family on p. 269 in *The Patterns of English Spelling* (TPES); the -eek, p. 408; the -eak, p. 408; the -eep, p. 424.

	89th day	90th day	91st day	92nd day
1.	weep	weeps	**wept**	weeping
2.	**sweep**	sweeps	**swept**	sweeping
3.	creep	creeps	crept	creeping
4.	peep	peeps	peeped	peeping
5.	seep	seeps	seeped	seeping
6.	steep	steeps	steeped	steeping
7.	**sheep**	**jeep**	jeeps	*** clothes**
8.	deep	deeper	deepest	deeply
9.	beep	beeps	beeped	beeping
10.	*** cheep**	cheeps	cheeped	cheeping
11.	*** cheap**	cheaper	cheapest	cheaply
12.	leap	leaps	leaped	leaping
13.	heap	heaps	heaped	heaping
14.	reap	reaps	reaped	reaping
15.	steeple	steeples	**aren't**	**doesn't**
16.	**people**	people's choice	**people**	people's voice
17.	pep	peps	pepped	pepping
18.	pepper	peppers	peppered	peppering
19.	step	steps	stepped	stepping
20.	misstep	missteps	instep	footsteps
21.	bicep	sidestep	tricep	forceps
22.	babe	babes	Babe Ruth	Babe Ruth's bat
23.	**baby**	**babies**	**babied**	**babying**
24.	**able**	unable	**ability**	disability
25.	disable	disables	disabled	disabling

* Homophones:

cheap/cheep   What do you call an inexpensive bird call? A cheap cheep.

close/clothes   We bought some new clothes at the close out sale.

See the complete -eep family on p. 424 in *The Patterns of English Spelling* (TPES); the -eap, p. 424; the -ep, p. 127; the -abe, p. 320; -able, p. 610; -ple, 612.

	93rd day	94th day	95th day	96th day
1.	enable	enables	enabled	enabling
2.	table	tables	tabled	tabling
3.	stable	stables	stability	inability
4.	cable	cables	cabled	cabling
5.	fable	fables	fabled	abilities
6.	gable	gables	gabled	disabilities
7.	sable	*** we're**	*** were**	*** (Am.) color**
8.	Bible	Bibles	**I'd**	**I've**
9.	noble	nobles	nobility	*** (Br.) colour**
10.	ruble	rubles	*** we're**	*** aunts**
11.	feeble	feebler	feeblest	**many**
12.	*** made**	shadow	shadows	shadowed
13.	shade	shades	shaded	shading
14.	*** wade**	wades	waded	wading
15.	fade	fades	faded	fading
16.	blade	blades	glade	glades
17.	trade	trades	traded	trading
18.	jade	jaded	trader	traders
19.	crusade	crusades	crusaded	crusading
20.	*** spade**	spades	crusader	crusaders
21.	persuade	persuades	persuaded	persuading
22.	lemonade	persuader	persuaders	persuasion
23.	invade	invaded	invading	invasion
24.	evade	evading	evaded	evasion
25.	abrade	abrades	abrasive	abrasion

* Homophones:

we're/were	We're going to go there. Were you ever there?
made/maid	Who made the bed? The maid.
wade/weighed	I like to wade into the water. He weighed a ton.
spade/spayed	You can dig with a spade. A dog may be spayed.
color/colour	In the United States, Americans color. In Great Britain, the British colour.
aunts/ants/aunt's	I have aunts and uncles. My aunt's pet ants were poisoned.

See the complete -ble family on p. 610 in TPES; the -ade, p. 321.

	97th day	98th day	99th day	100th day
1.	* **mail**	mails	mailed	mailing
2.	nail	nails	nailed	nailing
3.	snail	snails	sailor	sailors
4.	* **sail**	sails	sailed	sailing
5.	* **bail**	bails	bailed	bailing
6.	fail	fails	failed	failing
7.	* **Gail**	Gail's	failure	failures
8.	* **hail**	hails	hailed	hailing
9.	blackmail	blackmails	blackmailed	blackmailing
10.	* **pail**	pails	railroad	railroads
11.	rail	rails	railed	railing
12.	trail	trails	trailed	trailing
13.	* **male**	males	trailer	trailers
14.	female	females	**because**	my **aunt's** cat
15.	* **bale**	bales	baled	baling
16.	* **gale**	gales	(Am.) **color**	(Am.) **coloring**
17.	regale	regales	regaled	regaling
18.	* **hale**	been	(Br.) **colour**	(Br.) **colouring**
19.	inhale	inhales	inhaled	inhaling
20.	exhale	exhales	exhaled	exhaling
21.	* **sale**	sales	salesman	salesmen
22.	* **pale**	pales	paled	paling
23.	impale	impales	impaled	impaling
24.	Dale	Dale's	**before**	**before**
25.	scale	scales	scaled	scaling

* Homophones:

male/mail	What do you call letters for men only? Male mail.
sale/sail	What do you call a special on canvas? A sail sale.
bale/bail	You bale hay and cotton. You bail out a boat or post bail.
gale/Gail/Gayle	A gale is a wind storm. Gail's last name is Storm. So is Gayle's.
hale/hail	What do you call hearty ice? Hale hail.
pale/pail	What do you call a sick looking bucket? A pale pail.

See the complete -ale family on p. 422 in *The Patterns of English Spelling* (TPES); the -ail, p. 411.

	101st day	102nd day	103rd day	104th day
1.	derail	derails	derailed	derailing
2.	* tail	tails	before	* eye
3.	detail	details	detailed	detailing
4.	retail	retailer	retailers	* clothes
5.	cocktail	cocktails	quail	quails
6.	* wail	wails	wailed	wailing
7.	* whale	whales	whaler	whalers
8.	shale	stale	* tale	tales
9.	wholesale	wholesaler	wholesalers	tattletale
10.	* ale	ginger ale	ailment	ailments
11.	* ail	ails	ailed	ailing
12.	gal	gallons	gallop	galloped
13.	canal	canals	alley	alleys
14.	pal	pals	valley	valleys
15.	* rain	rains	rained	raining
16.	brain	brains	harebrained	rainy
17.	train	trains	trained	training
18.	grain	grains	trainer	trainers
19.	strain	strains	strained	straining
20.	* plain	plains	strainer	strainers
21.	restrain	restrains	restrained	restraining
22.	* lain	slain	restraint	restraints
23.	sprain	sprains	sprains	sprained
24.	gain	gains	gained	gaining
25.	drain	drains	drained	draining

* Homophones:

tail/tale	What do you call a story about a tail? A tail tale.
wail/whale	What do you call a cry by Moby Dick? A whale wail.
ail/ale	Ail means sick. Ale is a beverage.
lain/lane	Lie, lay, lain. A lane can be a path, street, or alley.
rain/rein/reign	During his reign, King Arthur had to rein in his knights when the rain came.
plain/plane	What's an ordinary aircraft? A plain plane.
I/eye/aye	I said "Aye, sir" not "eye sore"!
clothes/close	Please close the clothes closet door.

See the complete -ail family on p. 330 *The Patterns of English Spelling* (TPES); the -ale, p. 411; the -al, p. 146; the -ain, p. 419.

Sequential Spelling Level 2 - Teacher's Guide

	105th day	106th day	107th day	108th day
1.	* **pain**	pains	pained	paining
2.	explain	explains	explained	explaining
3.	* **vain**	explanation	explanations	explanatory
4.	complain	complains	complained	complaining
5.	Spain	Spain's plains	complaint	complaints
6.	stain	stains	stained	staining
7.	entertain	entertains	entertained	entertaining
8.	* **main**	mainly	entertainer	entertainment
9.	remain	remains	remained	remaining
10.	remainder	remainders	**can't**	**can't**
11.	* **ant**	ants	planter	planters
12.	plant	plants	planted	planting
13.	implant	implants	implanted	plantation
14.	slant	slants	slanted	slanting
15.	pant	pants	panted	panting
16.	rant	rants	ranted	ranting
17.	grant	grants	granted	granting
18.	chant	* **chants**	chanted	chanting
19.	enchant	enchants	enchanted	enchanting
20.	**want**	**wants**	**wanted**	**wanting**
21.	wad	wads	wadded	wadding
22.	quad	quads	squad	squads
23.	wand	wands	* **break**	**father**
24.	wander	wanders	wandered	wandering
25.	squander	squanders	squandered	squandering

* Homophones:

pane/pain	What do you call it when a window hurts? A pane pain.
vane/vain/vein	A weather vane. A vain person. A vein of gold (or a blood vessel).
mane/main/Maine	The hair on the back of a horse's neck is a mane. Maine is in New England.
	What is the difference between a main mane and a Maine mane?
	Who is the main man in Maine? Maine's governor.
ant/aunt	What do you call the wife of an ant's uncle? An ant aunt.
chants/chance	What do you call accidental songs? Chance chants.
break/brake	Give me a break. Take your foot off the brake.

See the complete -ain family on p. 419 in The Patterns of English Spelling (TPES); the -ant, p. 249, the –wa (wah) or –qua (KWah) p. 504.

	109th day	110th day	111th day	112th day
1.	**went**	pent	**spent**	penthouse
2.	vent	vents	vented	venting
3.	ventilate	ventilates	ventilated	ventilation
4.	event	events	eventual	eventually
5.	invent	invents	invented	inventing
6.	inventor	inventors	invention	inventions
7.	prevent	prevents	prevented	preventing
8.	* cent	* cents	prevention	preventative
9.	* scent	* scents	scented	scenting
10.	* sent	* we're	(Am.) colored	doesn't
11.	* assent	assents	assented	assenting
12.	* dissent	dissents	dissented	dissenting
13.	dissention	dissident	dissidents	* aunts
14.	* ascent	ascents	ascension	been
15.	* descent	descents	(Br.) coloured	before
16.	decent	decently	decency	decent
17.	absent	where	where	where
18.	tent	* tents	break-in	fathers
19.	intent	* intents¹	intentions	intentional
20.	Be con**tent**.	He con**tents** himself.	We are con**tent**ed.	contentment
21.	the **con**tent of	the **con**tents	eyeball	eyeful
22.	cement	cements	cemented	cementing
23.	We **lent** him $2.00.	Lenten	demented	aren't
24.	extent	extension	renter	renters
25.	**rent**	rents	rented	renting

* Homophones:

cent/scent/sent	What's a penny mailed? A sent cent. A cheap smell? A one cent scent.
cents/scents/sense	What's penny smarts? Cents sense. Smelling smarts? Scents sense.
assent/ascent	What's an agreement to go up? Ascent assent.
dissent/descent	What's a disagreement about going down? Descent dissent.
intense/intents/in tents	What are strong purposes inside Arab dwellings? Intense intents in tents.
tents/tense	What are uptight Arab dwellings? Tense tents.

See the complete -ent family on p. 250 in *The Patterns of English Spelling* (TPES).

¹The author once thought the phrase, "For all **intents and** purposes" was "For all **intensive** purposes!" Phrases such as "for all **intents** and purposes" that are heard more often than read can make for unusual misspellings that computers can't catch.

	113th day	114th day	115th day	116th day
1.	pint	pints	half pint	half pints
2.	print	* **prints**	printed	printing
3.	imprint	imprints	imprinted	imprinting
4.	misprint	misprints	misprinted	misprinting
5.	reprint	reprints	reprinted	reprinting
6.	hint	hints	hinted	hinting
7.	flint	flints	lint	winter
8.	glint	glints	glinted	glinting
9.	splint	splints	splinter	splinters
10.	sprint	sprints	sprinted	sprinting
11.	quint	* **quints**	sprinter	sprinters
12.	squint	squints	squinted	squinting
13.	tint	tints	tinted	tinting
14.	stint	stints	printer	printers
15.	mint	* **mints**	minted	minting
16.	**green**	greens	greener	greenest
17.	screen	screens	screened	screening
18.	wintergreen	* **seen**	sheen	keen
19.	colleen	colleens	teen	teens
20.	queen	queens	thirteen	fourteen
21.	**between**	in between	canteen	canteens
22.	Halloween	foreseen	fifteen	sixteen
23.	* **lean**	leans	leaned	leaning
24.	**clean**	cleans	cleaned	cleaning
25.	* **mean**	means	meant	meaning

* Homophones:

prince/prints	What does a king's son do when he writes? The prince prints.
quince/quints	What fruit is named after quintuplets. The quints' quince.
mince/mints	What means to chop up candies? Mince mints.
mean/mien	What do you call a bad attitude? A mean mien.
lean/lien	Bankers will lean toward attaching a lien on your property.
scene/seen	Have you seen the latest scene?

See the complete -int family on p. 251 in *The Patterns of English Spelling* (TPES); the -een, p. 420; the -ean, p. 420.

	117th day	118th day	119th day	120th day
1.	**mean**	meaner	meanest	meanly
2.	* **bean**	**beans**	beaned	beaning
3.	* Jean	**Jean's jeans**	dean	deans
4.	glean	gleans	gleaned	gleaning
5.	gleaner	gleaners	cleaners	cleanest
6.	wean	weans	weaned	weaning
7.	**have * been**	**has been**	**who'd**	**coming**
8.	**fine**	fines	* **fined**	fining
9.	define	defines	defined	defining
10.	nine	nines	definition	definitions
11.	canine	canines	definite	**definitely**
12.	refine	refines	refined	refining
13.	**pine**	pines	refinery	refinement
14.	confine	confines	confined	confining
15.	porcupine	porcupines	confinement	**dinner** in a diner
16.	**dine**	dines	dined	**dining room**
17.	**mine**	mines	* **mined**	mining
18.	undermine	undermined	* **miner**	undermining
19.	spine	spines	spinal	**clothes**
20.	vine	vines	final	**finally**
21.	divine	divinely	divinity	**hasn't**
22.	twine	twines	twined	twining
23.	**shine**	shines	shined/shone	**shining**
24.	sunshine	moonshine	swine	**haven't**
25.	* **whine**	whines	whined	whining

* Homophones:

been/bean	Depending on dialect spoken. My bean may have been broken.
been/bin	Depending on dialect spoken. My tool bin may have been messed up.
been/Ben	Depending on dialect spoken. Ben may have been there.
miner/minor	What is a young digger? A minor miner.
wine/whine	What is a cry for more of the grape? A wine whine.
Jean/Gene/gene	Jean wears blue jeans. Gene's genes were inherited.
fined/find	You may be fined if you find fault with the judge.
mined/mind	I hope you don't mind that I once mined for gold.

** Heteronyms:

Jean/Jean In English names, Jean rhymes with dean. In names from the French, like Jean Paul Trudeau, Jean ("ZHAWN") rhymes with lawn.

See the complete -ean family on p. 420 and the -ine on p. 337 in *The Patterns of English Spelling.*

Evaluation Test #3 (After 120 Days)

		Pattern being tested	Lesson word is in
1.	Do you know if their plane has arr**ived** yet?	ived	75
2.	Harry had a little l**amb** chop.	amb	77
3.	Our spelling should constantly be impr**oving**.	oving	80
4.	The gardener just tr**immed** the hedges.	immed	83
5.	We went tr**amping** through the countryside.	amping	84
6.	Did you get a new pair of sn**eakers**?	eakers	88
7.	Let a sl**eeping** dog lie.	eeping	88
8.	We just st**epped** over the little water puddle.	epped	91
9.	We gave him a h**eaping** helping of oatmeal.	eaping	92
10.	We sh**aded** our eyes from the blazing sun.	aded	95
11.	They were always tr**ading** baseball cards.	ading	96
12.	Have you ever been camping in a tr**ailer**?	ailer	99
13.	Inh**aling** second-hand smoke is bad for your health.	aling	100
14.	The team's tr**ainer** was held in high respect.	ainer	103
15.	I hate it when my sinuses are dr**aining**.	aining	104
16.	Have you ever seen an ench**anted** castle?	anted	107
17.	Our dog keeps w**andering** all around town.	andering	108
18.	Edison inv**ented** a lot of different things.	ented	111
19.	An ounce of prev**ention** is worth a pound of cure.	ention	111
20.	I hate getting spl**inters** in my fingers.	inters	116

	121st day	122nd day	123rd day	124th day
1.	outshine	outshines	outshined/outshone	outshining
2.	**dine**	diners	**been**	**before**
3.	brine	**dinners**	**father's**	**isn't**
4.	shrine	shrines	father-in-law	*** It's too cold.**
5.	combine	combines	combined	combining
6.	tine	tines	turpentine	combination
7.	**line**	lines	lined	**lining**
8.	underline	underlines	underlined	underlining
9.	Mr. Cline	liner	liners	recliner
10.	decline	declines	declined	declining
11.	incline	inclines	inclined	inclining
12.	equine	feline	bovine	inclination
13.	staff	staffs	staffed	staffing
14.	gaff	gaffs	gaffed	gaffing
15.	**laugh**	**laughs**	**laughed**	laughing
16.	Jeff	Jeff's	Mr. Neff	**laughter**
17.	**of**	**haven't**	*** four**	fours
18.	**off**	*** break**	break-in	**fourth**
19.	scoff	scoffs	scoffed	scoffing
20.	doff	doffs	doffed	doffing
21.	aft	**after**	rafter	rafters
22.	raft	rafts	rafted	rafting
23.	graft	grafts	grafted	grafting
24.	craft	crafts	crafted	a crafty person
25.	shaft	shafts	shafted	shafting

* Homophones:

it's/its   It's too bad your dog hurt its leg.

break/brake   It's no fun to break an arm. He stepped on the brake.

four/for   We will need four reservations for dinner

See the complete -ine family on p. 337 in *The Patterns of English Spelling* (TPES); the -aff, p. 141; the -eff, p. 142; the -off, p. 144; -aft, p. 232.

	125th day	126th day	127th day	128th day
1.	* **draft**	drafts	drafted	drafting
2.	* **draught**	draughts	draughted	draughting
3.	left	lefts	heft	hefty
4.	theft	thefts	bereft	heftier
5.	**eat**	**eats**	**ate/eaten**	**eating**
6.	* **beat**	**beats**	**beat/beaten**	**beating**
7.	* **feat**	**feats**	**who'd**	**aunt's**
8.	defeat	defeats	defeated	defeating
9.	**meat**	meats	fatherly	**It's too hot.**
10.	**peat**	who're	**heart**	**heart**
11.	repeat	repeats	repeated	repeating
12.	neat	wheat	repetitive	repetition
13.	fatherhood	* **fourth**	repetition	repetitive
14.	seat	seats	seated	seating
15.	cheat	cheats	cheated	cheating
16.	bleat	bleats	bleated	bleating
17.	pleat	pleats	pleated	pleating
18.	cleat	cleats	**treatment**	treatments
19.	treat	treats	treated	treating
20.	retreat	retreats	retreated	retreating
21.	**heat**	heats	heated	**heating**
22.	* **great**	* **greater**	**greatest**	**heaters**
23.	**sweat**	sweats	sweating	**sweaters**
24.	**threat**	threats	threat	threats
25.	**threaten**	threatens	**threatened**	threatening

* Homophones:

draft/draught   In the U.S., we draft soldiers, drink draft beer, and write drafts.
                        In England, they conscript soldiers, drink draught beer, and write draughts.
beat/beet   You can beat a drum. You can beat an egg. You can eat a beet.
feat/feet   Touching your nose with your toes is a feet feat.
fourth/forth   Going forth is not coming in fourth.
great/grate   It's great to charbroil a steak over a grate.
greater/grater   What do you need for better grated cheese? A greater grater.

See the complete -aft family on p. 232 in *The Patterns of English Spelling* (TPES); the -eft, p. 232; the -eat, p. 427.

	129th day	130th day	131st day	132nd day
1.	**date**	dates	dated	**dating**
2.	*** gate**	gates	**It's too** bad.	It hurt **its** paw.
3.	irrigate	irrigates	irrigating	irrigation
4.	irritate	irritates	irritating	irritation
5.	skate	skates	skated	**skating**
6.	**late**	**lately**	**later**	**latest**
7.	relate	related	relating	relation
8.	plate	plates	plated	relationship
9.	slate	slates	slated	relatives
10.	mate	mates	mated	mating
11.	cremate	cremated	cremating	cremation
12.	create	created	creating	creation
13.	*** grate**	*** grates**	grateful	gratefully
14.	*** great**	*** greats**	gratitude	ungrateful
15.	hate	hates	hating	hateful
16.	state	states	statement	station
17.	reinstate	reinstates	reinstatement	reinstating
18.	probate	probates	probating	probation
19.	vacate	vacated	vacating	**vacation**
20.	indicate	indicated	indicating	indication
21.	dedicate	dedicated	dedicating	dedication
22.	**locate**	located	locating	**location**
23.	**educate**	educated	educator	**education**
24.	validate	validated	validating	validation
25.	consolidate	consolidated	consolidating	consolidation

* Homophones:

gate/gait   If a gate could run, it would have a gate gait.

grate/great   What's the best thing to cook a steak on? A great grate.

grates/greats   Talking about military greats grates on my nerves.

See the complete -ate/-ation family on pages 347-353 in *The Patterns of English Spelling.*

	133rd day	134th day	135th day	136th day
1.	**timid**	timidity	timid	**timid**
2.	in**timid**ate	intimidated	intimidating	in**timid**ation
3.	accommodate	accommodated	accommodating	accommodations
4.	segregate	segregated	segregating	segregating
5.	congregate	congregated	congregating	congregating
6.	congress	congressman	congressmen	congressional
7.	obligate	obligates	obligating	obligation
8.	investigate	investigates	investigating	investigation
9.	appreciate	appreciates	appreciated	appreciation
10.	** **associate**	associated	associating	association
11.	radiate	radiated	radiating	radiation
12.	violate	violating	violator	violation
13.	isolate	isolated	isolating	isolation
14.	translate	translated	translator	translation
15.	calculate	calculated	calculator	calculation
16.	regulate	regulated	regular	regulation
17.	insulate	insulated	insulating	insulation
18.	congratulate	congratulated	congratulating	congratulations
19.	fascinate	fascinates	fascinating	fascination
20.	eliminate	eliminates	eliminating	elimination
21.	crime	crimes	criminal	criminals
22.	incriminate	incriminates	incriminating	incrimination
23.	discriminate	discriminates	discriminating	discrimination
24.	dominate	dominates	dominating	domination
25.	nominate	nominates	nominated	nomination

** Heteronyms:

associate ("uh SOH see AY't")   I associate with him.

associate ("uh SOH see it")   He is my associate.

                                I associate with my associates.

                                He associates with his associates.

See the complete -ate/ation family on pages 347-353; the -ate ("it") family on pages 354-355 in *The Patterns of English Spelling*.

	137th day	138th day	139th day	140th day
1.	donate	donated	donating	donations
2.	hibernate	hibernates	hibernating	hibernation
3.	take part	particle	particles	**clothes**
4.	participate	participates	participating	participation
5.	anticipate	anticipates	anticipating	anticipation
6.	** **separate**	separates	separated	separation
7.	** **separate** rooms	separately	separatism	separately
8.	celebrate	celebrates	celebrating	celebration
9.	vibrate	vibrates	vibrating	vibration
10.	liberate	liberates	liberating	liberation
11.	** to **deliberate**	deliberates	deliberating	deliberation
12.	** **deliberate**	deliberately	deliberate	deliberately
13.	**considerate**	considerately	considerate	considerately
14.	exaggerate	exaggerates	exaggerating	exaggeration
15.	refrigerate	refrigerator	refrigerators	refrigeration
16.	tolerate	tolerated	tolerant	toleration
17.	**operate**	operator	operators	operation
18.	cooperate	cooperates	cooperating	cooperation
19.	integrate	integrated	integrating	integration
20.	disintegrate	disintegrates	disintegrating	disintegration
21.	migrate	migrant	migratory	migration
22.	immigrate	immigrant	immigrating	immigration
23.	decorate	decorated	decorator	decoration
24.	vapor	vapors	evaporated	vaporize
25.	evaporate	evaporates	evaporating	evaporation

** **Heteronyms:**

separate ("SEP uh RAY't")   We should separate those two.
separate ("SEP rit")   We should put them in separate rooms.

deliberate ("duh LIB ur RAY't")   The jury needed more time to deliberate.
deliberate ("duh LIB ur rit")   It was no accident. It was a deliberate attempt to kill those weeds.

See the complete -ate/ation family on pages 347-353; the -ate ("it") family on pages 354-355 in *The Patterns of English Spelling*.

	141st day	142nd day	143rd day	144th day
1.	penetrate	penetrated	penetrating	penetration
2.	perpetrate	"perp" is slang	perpetrator	perpetration
3.	arbitrate	arbitrating	arbitrator	arbitration
4.	**concentrate**	concentrated	concentrating	**concentration**
5.	demonstrate	demonstrated	demonstrators	demonstration
6.	illustrate	illustrated	illustrating	illustration
7.	frustrate	frustrated	frustrating	**frustration**
8.	dictate	dictated	dictator	dictation
9.	**imitate**	imitated	imitating	**imitation**
10.	**irritate**	irritated	irritating	irritation
11.	**hesitate**	hesitated	hesitating	hesitation
12.	rotate	rotated	rotating	rotation
13.	amputate	amputated	amputating	amputation
14.	** graduate	graduated	graduating	**graduation**
15.	a ** **graduate** of	two graduates of	gradual	gradually
16.	evacuate	evacuated	evacuating	evacuation
17.	value	values	valued	valuing
18.	evaluate	evaluated	evaluating	evaluation
19.	insinuate	insinuated	insinuating	insinuation
20.	accentuate	accentuated	accentuating	accentuation
21.	punctuate	punctuated	punctuating	punctuation
22.	situate	situated	situating	**situation**
23.	equate	equating	equator	equation
24.	aggravate	aggravated	aggravating	aggravation
25.	elevate	elevated	elevator	elevation

**** Heteronyms:**

graduate ("GRAD joo AY't")   When are you going to graduate?

graduate ("GRAD joo it")   My brother is a graduate of Michigan State University.

See the complete -ate/ation family on pages 347-353; the -ate ("it") family on pages 354-355 in *The Patterns of English Spelling*.

	145th day	146th day	147th day	148th day
1.	**act**	**active**	**actor**	**action**
2.	activate	activated	activating	activation
3.	culture	cultures	agriculture	difficult
4.	cultivate	cultivated	cultivator	cultivation
5.	captive	captives	capture	captured
6.	captivate	captivated	captivating	captivation
7.	motive	motives	("moh TEEF") motif	motifs
8.	motivate	motivates	motivating	motivation
9.	**note**	notes	noted	noting
10.	footnote	footnotes	notable	notation
11.	denote	denotes	denoting	denotation
12.	connote	connotes	connoting	connotation
13.	quote	quotes	quoting	quotation
14.	misquote	misquoted	misquoting	misquotation
15.	**vote**	votes	voted	**voting**
16.	devote	devoted	devoting	devotion
17.	*** mote**	motes	motor	motion
18.	demote	demotes	demoted	demotion
19.	promote	promotes	promoted	promotion
20.	**by * rote**	He * **wrote** it.	He rewrote it.	writing
21.	**dote**	dotes	doted	doting
22.	antidote	antidotes	**tote**	totes
23.	anecdote	anecdotes	**total**	**totally**
24.	**private**	privates	privately	privacy
25.	delicate	delicates	delicately	delicately

* Homophones:

rote/wrote   He wrote what he had memorized or what he had learned by rote.

mote/moat   A speck of dust is a mote. Never go swimming in a moat.

See the complete -ate/ation family on pages 347-353; the -ate ("it") family on pages 354-355; the -ote/otion family on page 358 in *The Patterns of English Spelling*.

	149th day	150th day	151st day	152nd day
1.	media	media	media	media
2.	immediate	immediately	immediate	**immediately**
3.	my ** **associate**	my associates	**aren't**	**because**
4.	I ** **associate**	He associates	We're associating	association
5.	A ** **duplicate** key	Two duplicates	duplicated	**It's all right.**
6.	To ** **duplicate**	He duplicates	duplicating	duplication
7.	candid	candids	candidly	candidness
8.	candidate	candidates	candidacy	candidacy
9.	a ** **delegate**	many delegates	breaking	**quietly**
10.	I will ** **delegate**	He delegates	delegating	delegation
11.	very ** **appropriate**	appropriately	appropriate	appropriately
12.	We ** **appropriate**	appropriated	appropriation	appropriation
13.	chocolate	chocolates	**chocolate**	chocolates
14.	climate	climates	climate	climates
15.	obstinate	obstinately	obstinate	obstinately
16.	**fortune**	fortunes	*** you'll**	*** one**
17.	**fortunate**	fortunately	*** you're**	*** one-half**
18.	unfortunate	unfortunately	*** heart**	hearty
19.	pirate	pirates	pirating	piracy
20.	literate	literal	literally	literacy
21.	illiterate	illiterates	literature	illiteracy
22.	** **deliberate**	deliberately	** **deliberate**	deliberately
23.	We deliberated	he deliberates	deliberating	deliberation
24.	**accurate**	accurately	accuracy	inaccurate
25.	adequate	adequately	adequacy	inadequate

* Homophones:

you'll/Yule   Tell me how you'll celebrate Yule.

you're/your   You're going to love your test results.

one-half/won half   One-half of the contestants won half the two-man races.

** Heteronyms:

associate ("uh SOH see it") / associate ("uh SOH see AY't")   My associate will not associate with me.

duplicate ("DOO pluh kit") / duplicate ("DOO pluh KAY't")   In duplicate bridge you duplicate the hands.

appropriate ("uh PROH pree it") / appropriate ("uh PROH pree AY't")   It's not appropriate to appropriate my property.

delegate ("DEL uh git") / delegate ("DEL uh GAY't")   That delegate should delegate some of his work.

deliberate ("duh LIB ur it") / deliberate ("duh LIB ur AY't")   Be more deliberate when you deliberate.

See the complete -ate/ation family on pages 347-353; the -ate ("it") family on pages 354-355 in *The Patterns of English Spelling*.

	153rd day	154th day	155th day	156th day
1.	**age**	ages	aged	aging
2.	page	**pages**	paged	paging
3.	rampage	rampages	rampaged	rampaging
4.	cage	cages	caged	caging
5.	**rage**	rages	raged	raging
6.	enrage	enrages	enraged	enraging
7.	outrage	**outrageous**	outraged	outrageously
8.	**gauge**	gauges	gauged	gauging
9.	engage	engages	**engaged**	engagement
10.	disengage	disengaged	disengaging	disengagement
11.	sage	sages	crag	crags
12.	**stage**	stages	staged	staging
13.	**rag**	rags	ragged	ragging
14.	**bag**	bags	bagged	bagging
15.	**brag**	brags	**bragged**	**bragging**
16.	lag	lags	lagged	lagging
17.	**flag**	flags	flagged	flagging
18.	gag	gags	gagged	gagging
19.	nag	nags	**nagged**	**nagging**
20.	snag	snags	snagged	snagging
21.	sag	sags	sagged	sagging
22.	**tag**	tags	**tagged**	tagging
23.	wag	wags	**wagged**	**wagging**
24.	**drag**	drags	dragged	dragging
25.	zigzag	zigzags	zigzagged	zigzagging

See the complete -age family on p. 327 in *The Patterns of English Spelling* (TPES); the -ag, p. 111.

	157th day	158th day	159th day	160th day
1.	**bell**	bells	belled	belling
2.	dumbbell	dumbells	**fell**	**hello**
3.	jell	jells	jelly	Jell-o
4.	* **sell**	sells	sold	selling
5.	**tell**	tells	* **told**	**telling**
6.	foretell	foretells	foretold	foretelling
7.	**well**	wells	* **welled**	welling
8.	swell	swells	swelled	swelling
9.	dwell	dwells	dwelled	dwelling
10.	quell	quells	quelled	quelling
11.	smell	smells	smelled	smelling
12.	**spell**	spells	spelled	spelling
13.	misspell	misspells	**misspelled**	misspelling
14.	**shell**	shells	shelled	shelling
15.	* **cell**	cells	cellular	cellmate
16.	dell	dells	pell-mell	Nell
17.	**yell**	yells	yelled	yelling
18.	**yellow**	yellows	yellowed	yellowing
19.	bellow	bellows	bellowed	bellowing
20.	mellow	mellows	mellowed	mellowing
21.	**fellow**	fellows	swollen	droll
22.	* **roll**	rolls	rolled	rolling
23.	troll	trolls	trolled	trolling
24.	toll	tolls	* **tolled**	tolling
25.	stroll	strolls	strolled	strolling

* Homophones:

told/tolled	The poet told me that the bell tolled for all of us.
weld/welled	My son knows how to weld. Tears welled up in my eyes.
roll/role	What do you call a part in a play for a Danish? A roll role.
sell/cell	A salesman should know how to sell. A prison inmate lives in a cell.

See the complete -ell family on p. 149 in *The Patterns of English Spelling* (TPES); the -oll, p. 153.

Evaluation Test #4 (After 160 Days)

	Pattern being tested	Lesson word is in
1. Her new suit is at the cl**eaners**.	eaners	119
2. I can't stand people who are always wh**ining**.	ining	120
3. I'd like to float down the Mississippi on a r**aft**.	aft	121
4. I think I'd do it just for l**aughs**.	aughs	122
5. I like to be tr**eated** with some respect. Don't you?	eated	127
6. They bought each other matching sw**eaters**.	eaters	128
7. Not everybody loves to go ice sk**ating**.	ating	13
8. We didn't go anywhere on vac**ation**.	ation	132
9. Our house needs some new insul**ation**.	ation	136
10. He went to the hospital for an oper**ation**.	ation	140
11. Do you understand the situ**ation** that you're in?	ation	144
12. Husbands should be dev**oted** to their wives.	oted	146
13. I hope she gets the prom**otion**.	otion	148
14. Almost everybody loves chocol**ate**.	ate	149
15. Unfortun**ately**, some people can't eat sweets.	ately	150
16. The liter**acy** movement is gaining ground.	acy	152
17. The couple got eng**aged** on St. Valentine's Day.	aged	155
18. Nobody likes people who are always br**agging**.	agging	156
19. Nobody likes to missp**ell** a word.	ell	157
20. The injured elephant b**ellowed** long and loud.	ellowed	159

	161st day	162nd day	163rd day	164th day
1.	enroll	enrolls	enrolled	enrolling
2.	* **poll**	polls	polled	polling
3.	scroll	scrolls	scrolled	scrolling
4.	* **boll**	bolls	knoll	knolls
5.	troll	trolls	trolled	trolling
6.	**control**	controls	**controlled**	controlling
7.	decontrol	decontrols	decontrolled	decontrolling
8.	patrol	patrols	patrolled	patrolling
9.	extol	extols	extolled	extolling
10.	doll	dolls	all dolled up	dolly
11.	dolly	dollies	dollhouse	dollhouses
12.	loll	lolls	lolled	lolling
13.	folly	follies	lollipop	dollop
14.	**dull**	dulls	dulled	dulling
15.	gull	gulls	seagull	seagulls
16.	hull	hulls	hulled	hulling
17.	cull	culls	culled	culling
18.	lull	lulls	lulled	lulling
19.	lullaby	lullabies	skull	skulls
20.	mull	mulls	mulled	mulling
21.	**pull**	pulls	pulled	pulling
22.	**bull**	bulls	bully	bullies
23.	**full**	fully	pulley	pulleys
24.	**help**	helps	helped	helping
25.	yelp	yelps	yelped	yelping

* Homophones:

boll/bowl   A cotton boll. A bowl of cereal.

poll/pole   What do you call a questionnaire about poles? A pole poll.

See the complete -oll family on p. 153 in *The Patterns of English Spelling* (TPES); the -ol, p. 152; the -ull, p. 155; the -elp, p. 246.

	165th day	166th day	167th day	168th day
1.	helpless	helplessly	helplessness	*** your friend**
2.	helpful	helpfully	unhelpful	unhelpfully
3.	**bank**	banks	banked	banking
4.	**thank**	**thanks**	thanked	thanking
5.	lank	thankful	thankfully	bankers
6.	blank	blanks	blanked	blanking
7.	clank	clanks	clanked	clanking
8.	plank	planks	planked	planking
9.	flank	flanks	flanked	flanking
10.	**rank**	ranks	ranked	**ranking**
11.	crank	cranks	cranked	cranking
12.	frank	frankly	frankness	frankfurter
13.	prank	pranks	prankster	pranksters
14.	spank	spanks	spanked	spanking
15.	**tank**	tanks	tanker	tankers
16.	yank	yanks	yanked	yanking
17.	ankle	ankles	*** you're** nice	**you're quiet**
18.	rankle	rankles	rankled	rankling
19.	**ink**	inks	inked	inking
20.	**sink**	sinks	**sank/sunk**	**sinking**
21.	**drink**	**drinks**	**drank/drunk**	**drinking**
22.	shrink	shrinks	shrank/shrunk	shrinking
23.	stink	stinks	stank/stunk	stinking
24.	link	*** links**	linked	linking
25.	blink	blinks	blinked	**blinking**

* Homophones:

lynx/links   What do you call a golf course for wildcats? A lynx links.

you're/your   You're going to miss your plane if you don't hurry up.

See the complete -ank family on p. 220 in *The Patterns of English Spelling* (TPES); the -ink, p. 221; the -ankle, p. 605.

	169th day	170th day	171st day	172nd day
1.	slink	slinks	slinked	slinking
2.	**wink**	winks	winked	winking
3.	mink	minks	brink	brinks
4.	chink	chinks	chinked	chinking
5.	**think**	**thinks**	**thought**	**thinking**
6.	kink	kinks	kinked	kinking
7.	**pink**	pinks	**uncle**	**uncles**
8.	zinc	zinc	zinc	zinc
9.	link	links	linked	linking
10.	twinkle	twinkles	twinkled	twinkling
11.	**wrinkle**	wrinkles	**wrinkled**	wrinkling
12.	sprinkle	sprinkles	sprinkled	**sprinkling**
13.	sprinkler	sprinklers	blinker	blinkers
14.	**web**	webs	webbed feet	webbing
15.	ebb	ebbs	ebbed	ebbing
16.	cobweb	cobwebs	cobwebbed	spiderweb
17.	**leg**	**legs**	legging	leggings
18.	**beg**	**begs**	**begged**	**begging**
19.	peg	pegs	pegged	pegging
20.	**egg**	**eggs**	egged	egging
21.	keg	kegs	nutmeg	dregs
22.	honk	honks	honked	honking
23.	conk	conks	conked	conking
24.	donkey	donkeys	**hasn't**	**haven't**
25.	monk	monks	**monkey**	monkeys

See the complete -ink family on p. 221 in *The Patterns of English Spelling* (TPES); the -inkle, p. 605; the -eg, p. 112; the -onk, p. 222.

	173rd day	174th day	175th day	176th day
1.	**trunk**	trunks	drunk	drunks
2.	dunk	dunks	dunked	dunking
3.	bunk	bunks	bunked	bunking
4.	**junk**	junks	junked	junking
5.	plunk	plunks	plunked	plunking
6.	clunk	clunks	clunked	clunking
7.	flunk	flunks	flunked	flunking
8.	**sunk**	gunk	hunk	hunks
9.	chunk	chunks	slunk	**"thunk"**[1]
10.	**skunk**	skunks	**skunked**	skunking
11.	**uncle**	uncles	my **uncle's** car	**Uncle** Jim
12.	bookrack	gun rack	hat rack	hunchback
13.	tailback	swayback	touchback	hogback
14.	playback	cutback	feedback	drawback
15.	airsick	seasick	carsick	homesick
16.	toothpick	candlestick	joystick	lipstick
17.	shipwreck	bottleneck	roughneck	rubberneck
18.	paycheck	foredeck	fore-check	bodycheck
19.	o'clock	peacock	poppycock	deadlock
20.	hemlock	bedrock	livestock	oarlock
21.	roadblock	sunblock	shamrock	gridlock
22.	woodchuck	sawbuck	unstuck	potluck
23.	duckling	darling	starling	dumpling
24.	yearling	bedsprings	upswing	downswing
25.	herring	Wyoming	ringside	ringworm

See the complete -unk family on p. 222 in *The Patterns of English Spelling* (TPES); the -ack, p. 214; the -ick, p. 215; the -ock, p. 216; -uck, p. 216; -ing, p. 218.

[1] The word "*thunk*" is sometimes used by writers to indicate a dull metallic sound or as a nonstandard past tense of the word *think* (cf. *drink, drank, drunk* to *think, thank, "thunk"*). When a writer does the latter, it is usually humorous and also indicates the speaker is probably uneducated.

	177th day	178th day	179th day	180th day
1.	dedicated	two delegates	navy	radius
2.	dedication	delegated	navigate	radial
3.	indicating	delegation	navigator	radiate
4.	indication	valid	navigation	radiation
5.	medic	validate	irrigate	media
6.	medicine	validation	irrigation	mediate
7.	medicinal	timid	irritate	mediator
8.	medical	intimidate	irritating	mediation
9.	medicated	intimidation	irritation	immediate
10.	medication	commode	investigate	immediately
11.	implicate	commodity	investigator	remediate
12.	implicated	accommodate	investigating	remedial
13.	implications	accommodating	investigations	remediation
14.	** syndicate	accommodations	negotiate	fury
15.	syndicated	create	negotiated	furies
16.	syndication	creating	negotiating	furious
17.	complicated	creation	negotiations	infuriate
18.	complications	oblige	appreciate	infuriated
19.	communicate	obliged	appreciated	abbreviate
20.	communicating	obligated	appreciation	abbreviated
21.	communications	obligations	office	abbreviation
22.	lubricated	congregate	officer	alleviate
23.	lubrication	congregated	official	alleviated
24.	educated	congregating	officiate	alleviating
25.	education	congregation	officiating	alleviation

** Heteronyms:
syndicate ("SIN duh kit") / syndicate ("sin duh KAY't")   A syndicate may syndicate cartoons.

See the complete -ate family on p. 347 in *The Patterns of English Spelling* (TPES).

Final Evaluation Test

		Pattern being tested	Lesson word is in
1.	My neighbor has a lot of neph**ews** and nieces.	ews	2
2.	It finally d**awned** on me that I goofed.	awned	7
3.	My neighbor makes a living t**uning** pianos.	uning	12
4.	I was h**oping** that you would ask that question.	oping	16
5.	I hope everybody is rel**axed** and enjoying this test.	axed	27
6.	We had to get our old t**oaster** repaired.	oaster	32
7.	I wish you would stop h**umming** that song.	umming	44
8.	We scr**ubbed** and waxed the floor.	ubbed	59
9.	They bought a used car inst**ead** of a new one.	ead	63
10.	I know that you all are impr**oving** your spelling.	oving	80
11.	I hope I am not st**epping** on anybody's toes.	epping	92
12.	Does anybody know who inv**ented** television?	ented	111
13.	An ounce of prev**ention** is worth a pound of cure.	ention	111
14.	I have to stop by the cl**eaners** on the way home.	eaners	119
15.	They tr**eated** us as if we were royalty.	eated	127
16.	I think that they are sk**ating** on thin ice.	ating	132
17.	This situ**ation** calls for tact and diplomacy.	ation	144
18.	Did your sister get the prom**otion**?	otion	148
19.	Let others do the br**agging** for you.	agging	156
20.	I'm glad we all contr**olled** our tempers.	olled	163
21.	Very few people are completely h**elp**less.	elp	165
22.	We should all be th**ank**ful.	ank	166
23.	The lawyer had a tw**inkle** in her eye.	inkle	169
24.	The defendant b**egged** the judge for mercy.	egged	171
25.	The car was totaled. So we j**unked** it.	unked	175

Day 2

Unscramble these:

1. hewcs   **chews**
2. rwsec   **screws**
3. rbew   **brew**
4. wrde   **drew**
5. rsewne   **renews**
6. spneehw   **nephews**
7. awcsl   **claws**
8. wahts   **thaws**
9. srawts   **straws**

Day 3

Fill in the blank:

1. Oh no! My dog just **chewed** my sock!
2. I **knew** that we would be late today because it snowed last night.
3. My dad **brewed** the coffee this morning. Usually my mom **brews** it.
4. I'm having an **awful** day. How is yours?
5. Ouch! Leslie's cat just **clawed** me!
6. Jack **withdrew** from the race because he sprained his ankle.
7. We went the library and **renewed** our library cards today.
8. At summer camp we all got a **few** mosquito bites, but Jane had the fewest.
9. The oil well **blew** and **spewed** oil into the ocean.
10. Has the ice on the lake **thawed** yet? If not, let's go ice skating.

Day 4

Can You Find the Words?

```
+  +  +  +  +  F  +  +  +  W  +  +  S  +  +
+  +  +  +  L  D  +  +  +  E  +  +  R  +  +
+  +  +  A  E  +  +  C  +  L  +  +  E  +  +
+  +  W  W  +  +  +  +  L  B  +  +  W  +  +
+  E  E  +  +  +  +  +  A  +  A  +  A  +  +
D  R  +  +  W  Y  L  L  U  F  W  A  R  +  +
B  N  E  P  H  E  W  +  W  N  +  E  D  +  +
S  W  E  R  H  T  H  E  +  E  +  D  D  +  +
K  +  G  +  +  N  C  W  +  +  +  +  +  +  +
E  D  +  N  +  K  +  +  +  +  +  +  +  +  +
W  +  R  +  I  +  +  +  +  +  +  +  +  +  +
E  +  +  A  +  W  P  A  W  S  +  +  +  +  +
D  +  +  +  W  +  A  +  +  +  +  +  +  +  +
+  +  +  +  +  +  +  H  +  +  +  +  +  +  +
+  +  +  +  +  +  +  +  T  +  +  +  +  +  +
```

(Over, Down, Direction)

AWFULLY(12,6,W)   FLAWED(6,1,SW)
BLEW(10,4,N)   KNEW(6,10,NE)
BREWED(1,7,NE)   NEPHEW(2,7,E)
CHEW(8,9,NW)   NEW(10,7,S)
CLAWED(8,3,SE)   PAWS(7,12,E)
DRAW(2,10,SE)   SKEWED(1,8,S)
DRAWERS(13,7,N)   THAWING(9,15,NW)
   THREW(6,8,W)

Day 5

Fill in the blank:

1. It's your job to mow the **lawn**, not mine!
2. **Dawn** is the beginning of a new day.
3. We need to **calk (caulk)** the windows so the cold air doesn't get in. **Calk (caulk)** may also be spelled **caulk (calk)**.
4. Let's a piece of chalk to write on the **sidewalk**.
5. The umpire called that move a **balk** so the runner went to second base.
6. **Silk** thread is spun by **silk**worms.
7. It's a long **walk** to school.
8. When they did the wash, pioneer women had to **wring** the clothes by hand.
9. Did you hear the bells **ring**?
10. **Milk** is a good source of calcium, along with other dairy products.

Day 6

Unscramble these:

1. ssakwield   **sidewalks**
2. wardkylaw   **awkwardly**
3. naysw   **yawns**
4. asMhkwo   **Mohawks**
5. rsgwni   **wrings**
6. sgnsi   **sings**
7. naswl   **lawns**
8. lsbak   **balks**
9. ckusla   **caulks**
10. saclk   **calks**

Day 8

Can You Find the Words?

```
+  S  S  K  L  A  W  E  D  I  S  +  +  +  G
+  +  I  +  +  D  C  +  +  +  +  +  +  N  +
+  +  +  N  E  +  +  H  +  +  +  +  I  G  +
+  +  +  K  G  +  G  +  A  +  K  A  +  +  +
+  +  L  +  +  S  N  +  +  L  L  W  +  H  +
Y  A  W  A  L  K  I  N  G  U  K  +  +  A  +
T  L  A  W  N  S  K  +  A  I  +  E  +  W  +
G  +  D  +  +  +  L  C  N  +  +  +  D  K  +
+  N  +  R  +  +  A  G  +  +  +  +  +  I  S
+  +  I  +  A  +  T  +  +  +  +  +  +  N  G
+  +  +  N  +  W  S  G  N  I  R  P  S  G  N
+  +  +  +  W  +  K  +  +  +  +  +  +  +  I
+  +  +  +  +  A  +  W  +  +  +  +  +  +  R
+  +  +  +  +  +  +  +  A  +  +  +  +  +  W
+  +  +  +  +  +  +  +  +  +  +  +  +  +  +
```

(Over, Down, Direction)
AWKWARDLY(9,14,NW)
AWNING(6,13,NW)
CAULKING(8,8,NE)
CHALKED(7,2,SE)
GAWKING(14,3,SW)
HAWKING(14,5,S)
LAWNS(2,7,E)
SIDEWALKS(11,1,W)
SINGS(2,1,SE)
SPRINGS(13,11,W)
STALKING(7,11,N)
TALKED(1,7,NE)
WALKING(3,6,E)
WRINGS(15,14,N)

Day 9

Verb conjugations:

ring, rang, rung
bring, brought, brought
swing, swung, swung

Sentences showing understanding of proper verb tense are appropriate.

Day 10

Fill in the blank:

1. The wet paper **clings** to the glass.
2. The **strings** of white lights are very lovely.
3. I took **everything** out of my backpack to see if I could find my cell phone.
4. Wow! My little brother was yelling at the top of his **lungs**.
5. Have you ever skipped **stones** on a pond? It's fun!
6. Sometimes, being an only child can be very **lonely**.
7. The Pacific Ocean spawns **cyclones**. The Atlantic Ocean spawns hurricanes.
8. A hummingbird beats its **wings** very fast.
9. A witness in a trial is sometimes granted **immunity** from prosecution.
10. Sue and Lisa went to **swing** on the **swings**.

Day 13

Unscramble these:

1. ruepn   **prune**
2. deun   **dune**
3. osple   **slope**
4. mucneom   **commune**
5. hpeo   **hope**
6. eopel   **elope**
7. telopeces   **telescope**
8. tporenopu   **opportune**
9. ocpes   **scope**
10. opme   **mope**

Day 14

Fill in the blank:

1. Do you eat **prunes** for breakfast?
2. We went to the **community** center for the party.
3. I hope we have an **opportunity** to ask questions.
4. Jon and Jake went for a hike on the **dunes**.
5. Please hold onto these **ropes** for me.
6. Can you see Pluto through this **telescope**?
7. Ouch! My sprained ankle really **throbs**!
8. Oops! How many **blobs** of jam did you drop on your paper?
9. The policeman said that the two **robbers** were caught yesterday.
10. It was a **mob** scene at the concert.

Day 16

```
+  +  +  +  +  +  G  +  +  +  +  +  L  C  T
O  P  P  O  R  T  U  N  I  T  Y  O  O  G  E
M  E  R  +  +  +  +  +  I  +  B  M  +  N  L
+  I  P  O  +  +  +  +  +  B  M  +  U  I  E
H  +  C  O  B  +  +  +  Y  U  B  T  +  B  S
O  +  +  R  R  B  +  +  N  +  P  O  +  B  C
P  +  +  +  O  +  E  I  +  E  +  +  M  O  O
I  +  +  +  +  S  T  D  N  +  +  +  +  B  P
N  +  +  +  +  Y  C  +  +  +  +  +  +  +  E
G  +  G  N  I  B  B  O  R  H  T  +  +  +  +
+  E  P  O  H  +  +  +  P  +  +  +  +  +  +
+  +  +  +  +  +  +  +  +  E  +  +  +  +  +
+  +  +  +  +  +  +  +  +  +  +  +  +  +  +
S  L  O  P  I  N  G  +  +  +  +  +  +  +  +
+  +  +  +  +  +  +  +  +  +  +  +  +  +  +
```

(Over, Down, Direction)
BOBBING(14,8,N)
COMMUNITY(14,1,SW)
HOPE(5,11,W)
HOPING(1,5,S)
LOBBY(13,1,SW)
MICROSCOPE(1,3,SE)
MOBBING(13,7,NW)
NEPTUNE(9,8,NE)
OPPORTUNITY(1,2,E)
ROBBED(3,3,SE)
ROPE(5,6,NW)
SLOPING(1,14,E)
TELESCOPE(15,1,S)
THROBBING(11,10,W)

Day 17

Unscramble these

1. rjeciskah   **hijackers**
2. canrgitk   **tracking**
3. kaedtc   **tacked**
4. nlk igac   **lacking**
5. anigcpk   **packing**
6. rsrckaec   **crackers**
7. akncgrci   **cracking**
8. atadekct   **attacked**
9. ekdcas   **sacked**
10. kqacdue   **quacked**

Day 21

Fill in the blank:

1. I will send a **check** to pay the bill today.
2. The tow truck hauled the **wreck** away.
3. There is a **fleck** of gold in the fabric.
4. To go to the next web page, **click** here.
5. That's a really good **trick**! Where did you learn it?
6. Jake poked the leaves with a **stick** and the snake slithered out.
7. The nurse needs to **prick** your finger for the blood test.
8. What a **kick**! It went straight through the goalposts!
9. Before you light the candle, you need to trim the **wick**.
10. Last week, our family was **sick** with the flu.

Day 24

Unscramble these:

1. ghiencck   **checking**
2. yslresklec   **recklessly**
3. eewkcrr   **wrecker**
4. ckerhces   **checkers**
5. cdicelk   **clicked**
6. kccnankkik   **knickknack**
7. cchniek   **chicken**
8. cpkdee   **pecked**
9. ikrcfligne   **flickering**
10. siekctqu   **quickest**

Day 25

Fill in the blanks:

1. Can you **coax** the cat to come down from the tree?
2. Would you like waffles for **breakfast**?
3. How **fast** can you get here? We need to leave in ten minutes.
4. Did you hear the **broadcast** of the hockey game?
5. Jack was the **last** person to leave.
6. What color **sox (socks)** are you wearing today?
7. Did you put the **box** of crackers away?
8. We like to go to the lake in the summer to **relax**.
9. Can your dad **fix** the leak in the sink?
10. Does your mom **wax** the floor anymore? Mine doesn't.

Day 26

1. brsdaacots   **broadcasts**
2. exemris   **remixes**
3. samt   **mast**
4. ipxerefs   **prefixes**
5. ousfoxte   **outfoxes**
6. xeocsa   **coaxes**
7. nexo   **oxen**
8. xmiers   **mixers**
9. exas   **axes**
10. eswax   **waxes**

Day 30

Fill in the blank:

1. The tugboat captain blew three **blasts** on the whistle as we came into the harbor.
2. People who live in the **eastern** United States are called **Easterners**.
3. Do the colors stay **consistent** on your computer screen?
4. I can't **resist** the smell of freshly baked chocolate chip cookies.
5. Making **lists** helps me stay organized. How about you?
6. On Wednesdays, lunch **consists** of a peanut butter sandwich.
7. Allison is going to be Mr. Brown's **assistant**.
8. The doctor was **insistent** that my mom get an x-ray today.
9. My mom usually cooks two **roasts** for Sunday dinner.
10. Our favorite sandwich on Saturday is **toasted** cheese.

Day 34

Fill in the blank:

1. Did you get **lost** while you were hiking yesterday?
2. What is that **musty** smell?
3. How many **streams** do we have to cross on the way to the campground?
4. Lisa makes really good ice **cream**.
5. The space shuttle **burst** through the cloud layer when it landed.
6. With two powerful **thrusts** of his legs, the diver pushed off of the ocean floor.
7. How many **reams** of paper do we need to order?
8. Her **screams** helped us find her quickly.
9. How strong were the wind **gusts** yesterday?
10. Our food **costs** have increased this year.

Day 35

Unscramble these:

1. otaedcsc   **accosted**
2. oyclts   **costly**
3. asumdtr   **mustard**
4. dtseud   **dusted**
5. dsaermce   **screamed**
6. tseiusgdd   **disgusted**
7. edtemsa   **steamed**
8. urysct   **crusty**
9. ddtaeruejs   **readjusted**
10. daemeb   **beamed**

Day 36

```
+ + + + + + + + G + D + D + +
+ + C + S + + N + + R + E G +
T H R U S T I N G D A C F N +
+ + + S T R + R + T O R I +
+ + + S T D E R + S S O T +
+ + + U + E A O A + U T S S +
+ + J + M M B R + M M L T U +
+ D + A I U + + D + I Y E G +
A + E N S + + + + + N D S +
+ R G T G U S H I N G + G I +
C + + S + + + + + + + D + +
+ + + + + O + G N I T S R U B
+ + + + + + C + + + + + + +
+ + + + + + C + + + + + +
+ + + + + + + A + + + + + +
```

(Over,Down,Direction)
ACCOSTED(9,15,NW)
ADJUSTING(1,9,NE)
BURSTING(15,12,W)
COSTLY(12,3,S)
CREAMED(1,11,NE)
CUSTARD(3,2,SE)
DEFROSTED(13,1,S)

DISGUSTING(14,11,N)
DREAMING(10,3,SW)
GUSHING(5,10,E)
MUSTARD(11,7,N)
ROBUST(9,5,SW)
STREAMING(5,2,SE)
THRUSTING(1,3,E)

Day 37

Fill in the blanks:

1. Our **team** is wearing blue and white.
2. Sewing a curved **seam** is harder than sewing a straight one.
3. I'll take the **blame** for the broken window.
4. Would you like to play a **game** with me?
5. What is the **name** of that song?
6. Personally, I think it is a terrible **shame**.
7. Should we wait for **them** to get here?
8. What part of the country are you f**rom**?
9. We need to speak out and **condemn** this violence.
10. Do you have a **nickname**?

Day 40

```
Y C + G + + + N + + + + + + +
L O + + N + + O G N I M A L B
S N + + + I + I + + + + + + +
U D + + + + M T + + + + S +
O E N I C K N A M I N G T + M
M M + + + + + N E + + E + E S
A N + + B + H M + R M + H S +
F I + + O E + E + M D Y E + +
+ N G + M + G D I + A R + + +
+ G N M B N + N + M T + + + +
+ + I + I + G O A S H A M E D
+ N M M N + + C M + + + + + +
G + A + G E M A C R E V O + +
+ E L + + + E + + + + + + + +
T + F + + S + + + + + + + + +
```

(Over,Down,Direction)
ASHAMED(9,11,E)
BLAMING(15,2,W)
BOMBING(5,7,S)
CONDEMNATION(8,12,N)
CONDEMNING(2,1,S)
DREAMING(11,8,NW)
FAMOUSLY(1,8,N)

FLAMING(3,15,N)
HEMMING(7,7,SW)
MAYHEM(10,10,NE)
NICKNAMING(3,5,E)
OVERCAME(13,13,W)
SEAMSTRESS(6,15,NE)
STEMMING(14,4,SW)
TEAMING(1,15,NE)

Day 41

Fill in the blank:

1. My **father** and **mother** met in college.
2. I have **faith** in you. Keep it up!
3. Emily's **brother** left for college this fall.
4. **Math** has always been a difficult subject for me.
5. To get to the soccer game, you need go **south** on Elm Street for two blocks.
6. I was sorry to hear of your grandfather's **death**. Was he in poor health for a long time?
7. There are a **wealth** of job opportunities with a computer technology degree.
8. To **sum** it up, we lost the game.
9. Jack needs to give his dog a **bath**.
10. Please put a **cover** over the bread so it can rise.

Day 47

Unscramble these

1. udedmmr   **drummed**
2. mhmdceu   **chummed**
3. mdmrer   **drummer**
4. purbmel   **plumber**
5. ctehlos   **clothes**
6. nuocmmno   **uncommon**
7. heundns   **shunned**
8. estnndu   **stunned**
9. nneo   **none**
10. onabc   **bacon**

Day 50

Fill in the blank:

1. How many **cartons** of **melons** did you unload from the truck
2. There were several **reasons** we missed the flight. One of them was traffic near the airport.
3. How **many** people are you expecting for the party?
4. Lisa is **all done** with her project.
5. Emily **prefers** to sit in the passenger seat.
6. We had several **offers** of help with designing the scenery for the musical.
7. Cleaning fluid and ammonia are **poisons**.
8. Which of the four **seasons** do you **prefer**?
9. A prisoner can appeal to the president for a **pardon**.
10. Did you practice your trombone **lesson**?

Day 52

```
S + + + + + G + + G + + + S +
R + + + G N I N N U D + + N +
E + + + + + + I I + + + + O +
N + + + + R + + N + + + S +
O + + + + R + + + O + + A +
S + + + E + + + + S S + E +
I + S F + + + + + T + A R +
R O E E + W H I R R I N G E +
P R F + H + + N + B R + + + S
+ I + F + T O + E + R + + + +
+ + S + E S O C + + I + + + +
+ + + L A R A L + + N + + M +
+ + + E A U I + C + G + + A +
+ + R + S N + N W E A P O N S
+ T E E + + D + G + + + + Y +
```

(Over,Down,Direction)

BECAUSE(10,9,SW)
CLOTHES(9,13,NW)
DUNNING(11,2,W)
ISLAND(2,10,SE)
MANY(14,12,S)
OFFERING(2,8,SE)
PRISONERS(1,9,N)

REASONS(14,7,N)
REFERRING(2,9,NE)
SEASONING(15,9,NW)
STIRRING(11,6,S)
TREASON(2,15,NE)
WEAPONS(9,14,E)
WHIRRING(6,8,E)

Day 53
Fill in the blank:

1. I took a **cab** to the airport.
2. Let's **grab** a bite to eat.
3. Some students go to **school** at home.
4. We have **different** opinions on many things.
5. From the evidence left behind, you could **infer** that the culprit was the dog.
6. My mom and dad usually **confer** about our summer vacation destination.
7. Each fall, we **transfer** our summer clothes to a different closet.
8. For a July day, it's pretty **cool**.
9. When it's hot, I really like to go to the **pool**.
10. That color is rather **drab**; could you pick something else?

Day 54
Answers will vary.

Day 55

1. brycab   **crabby**
2. bgbary   **grabby**
3. nfartreedsr   **transferred**
4. nredierf   **inferred**
5. ndefrficee   **difference**
6. sonhecdulo   **unschooled**
7. epsdloo   **spooled**
8. roledod   **drooled**
9. dbestba   **stabbed**
10. debbda   **dabbed**

Day 60

```
+ + + + + + + + + + + + P R
Y L I D A E T S + + + + I + E
B L A C K H E A D S + E + Y J
+ G + P + P P + + + C + L G O
+ + N + E L I G + E + L + N I
+ + + I E A N E M + U + + I C
+ + + A L I C E C F + + + D I
C + S + D I A E D I + + A N
H E + I + L O A F + N + + E G
O + O + + + E R + U + G + R +
I V + + + R + + B + L + + T +
C + + + D + + + B O I L I N G
E + + + + + S A E P + + Y + +
S + + + + + + + + + + + + +
+ + + + + + + + + + + + + +
```

(Over,Down,Direction)

BLACKHEADS(1,3,E)
BOILING(9,12,E)
BROILING(9,11,NW)
CHOICES(1,8,S)
DREADFULLY(5,12,NE)
PEACEFULLY(4,4,SE)
PEAS(10,13,W)

PIECEMEAL(14,1,SW)
PIECING(6,4,SE)
PLEASE(7,4,SW)
REJOICING(15,1,S)
STEADILY(8,2,W)
TREADING(14,11,N)
VOIDING(2,11,NE)

Day 64
Unscramble these:

1. nrdweodntdo   **downtrodden**
2. caepe   **peace**
3. eemacepil   **piecemeal**
4. edheaadd   **deadhead**
5. cigivnion   **invoicing**
6. doluiellc   **celluloid**
7. inirolgb   **broiling**
8. adlsiyte   **steadily**
9. udlaryldfe   **dreadfully**
10. iginpec   **piecing**

Day 68

```
+ + + + + + + D L I O M R U T G
+ + + + + + + E + + + + + + N +
A P P O I N T I N G + + I + +
C + + + + + N + D + + D + + +
S L + + + T I + + U W + T + R
N T O + + O O + + O O N + E D
I E + T + I P Y R + E L J + E
O N + + H L P C R M + O A + L
J D + + + E A + T T I + + + I
+ E + + + T S N + N E + + + O
+ R + + + S I + I + + L + + C
+ L + + + O D N + + + + I + E
+ O + + P + G + + + + + + O R
+ I + P T S E I D U O L C + T
+ N A S H R O U D E D + + + +
```

(Over,Down,Direction)
ALOUD(13,8,NW)
APPOINTING(1,3,E)
APPOINTMENT(3,15,NE)
CLOTHES(1,4,SE)
CLOUDIEST(13,14,W)
CROWDING(8,8,NE)
DISAPPOINTED(7,12,N)
JOINS(1,9,N)

RECOILED(15,13,N)
REJOINING(15,5,SW)
SHROUDED(4,15,E)
TENDERLOIN(2,6,S)
TOILETRY(15,14,NW)
TOILETS(6,5,S)
TURMOIL(14,1,W)

Day 71

Fill in the blank:
1. **I'd** like to invite you to my party on Friday. Can you come?
2. Lisa won't be there **because** she is going to be out of town.
3. How **many** weeks are left in the year?
4. Do you like my **playhouse**? My dad built it for me.
5. Thanks for loaning me your umbrella. You're a **lifesaver**!
6. Allison and Julie **braved** the cold to walk to school.
7. My grandmother **gave** me that **engraved** bracelet for my birthday.
8. I'm sorry you have to leave. We were **having** such a good time!
9. Jack **waved** from the other side of the room.
10. Even though they are two years old, the twins are very well **behaved**.

Day 74

```
+ + + + + E + S Y + + + + + + B
S + + + V + S + L + + + + E +
H + + + A + E + + E + + C D
A + + + G + N + S + V A + E +
V + + + R + L B + A U A V + G
I N + + O + U + L S V A R N +
N + + + F + F + E O H I I B R
G E L S I + H + + E U V N + A
+ + + + + + T + B + A S + G V
+ + G N I S U O H H + + I + I
+ + + M + O + E + + + + N N
+ + A + + Y B D O U S I N G
+ + N + + + S + + + + + + + +
+ Y + + + I + + + + + + + + +
+ + + + M G U A R D H O U S E
```

(Over,Down,Direction)
BECAUSE(15,1,SW)
BEHAVED(9,9,NE)
BLOUSING(8,5,SE)
BRAVELY(14,7,NW)
DOUSING(9,12,E)
FORGAVE(5,7,N)
GUARDHOUSE(6,15,E)

HOUSING(9,10,W)
ISLE(5,8,W)
MANY(5,11,SW)
MISBEHAVING(5,15,NE)
RAVING(15,7,S)
SAVING(9,4,SE)
SHAVING(1,2,S)
YOUTHFULNESS(7,12,N)

Day 76

Unscramble these:
1. teeifass **safeties**
2. anlvirelg **ravelling**
3. ngeratliv **traveling**
4. liielekf **lifelike**
5. nvggii **giving**
6. iilnvg **living**
7. vainirrg **arriving**
8. ivler **liver**
9. nieskv **knives**
10. uvrevsi **survive**

Day 77

Unscramble these:
1. ieomv **movie**
2. oerpv **prove**
3. mevo **move**
4. vmeeor **remove**
5. periovm **improve**
6. mard **dram**
7. blam **lamb**
8. alms **slam**
9. ridsopavpe **disapprove**
10. dma **dam**

Day 78

```
+  +  +  M  +  +  D  +  G  +  I  +  D  +  G
+  +  A  +  +  A  +  N  +  M  R  +  I  +  N
+  L  +  +  M  +  I  +  P  +  A  +  S  +  I
C  +  G  M  +  M  G  R  A  M  M  +  A  +  M
+  +  I  N  M  S  O  +  +  +  M  +  P  +  M
+  N  +  A  I  V  T  S  +  +  I  +  P  +  A
G  +  L  +  E  V  +  R  M  +  N  +  R  +  R
+  S  +  M  +  +  I  +  I  A  G  +  O  +  C
+  +  E  +  +  +  +  R  +  V  R  +  V  +  +
+  N  +  +  +  +  +  P  +  I  T  I  +  +
T  H  R  I  V  I  N  G  +  E  +  N  N  M  +
G  N  I  V  O  R  P  P  A  +  D  +  G  A  +
+  +  +  +  +  G  N  I  V  O  M  +  +  W  +
+  +  +  +  +  +  +  +  +  +  +  +  +  S  +
+  +  +  +  +  +  +  +  +  +  +  +  +  +  +
```

(Over, Down, Direction)

APPROVING(9,12,W)   IMPROVEMENT(11,1,SW)
CLAM(1,4,NE)   MOVING(11,13,W)
CRAMMING(15,8,N)   RAMMING(11,2,S)
DAMMING(7,1,SW)   SLAMMING(2,8,NE)
DEPRIVING(11,12,NW)   STRIVING(6,5,SE)
DISAPPROVING(13,1,S)   SWAM(14,14,N)
GRAM(7,4,E)   THRIVING(1,11,E)
                           TRAMS(12,10,NW)

Day 81

Fill in the blank:

1. What is your favorite **hymn**?
2. On a **whim**, we went for a **swim** in the lake.
3. I like to drink **skim** milk with my cereal.
4. My mom would like a new **lamp** for the living room.
5. After the accident, the police decided to **clamp** down on speeding drivers.
6. The **champ** gave autographs at the hardware store yesterday.
7. Please bring me a **stamp** for this letter. Thanks!
8. If you don't drink enough water, it can cause a **cramp**.
9. Will you be going to **cramp** this summer?
10. Unless we can fix the problem, the future looks **grim**.

Day 86

Fill in the blank:

1. The rain put a **damper** on our picnic.
2. The mountain **peaks** in Colorado were beautiful.
3. Did you hear those **creaks** on the stairs?
4. The plumber came to fix the **leaks** in the sink yesterday.
5. Jake fell **asleep** in the chair last night.
6. Did you ask your parents if you could **keep** the puppy?
7. In the fall, a chipmunk's **cheeks** are full of nuts.
8. Did you hear those **shrieks**? They were coming from over there.
9. The sound is getting **weaker**. We're moving away from it.
10. Bobby had **streaks** of dirt on his face.

Day 87

Write the words that make up the contraction.

1. we're   **we are**
2. you're   **you are**
3. they're   **they are**
4. I'm   **I am**
5. we've   **we have**
6. you've   **you have**
7. I've   **I have**
8. I'll   **I will**
9. you'll   **you will**
10. we'll   **we will**
11. she'll   **she will**
12. he'll   **he will**
13. aren't   **are not**

Day 91

Fill in the blank:

1. I **wept** when I saw the damage to our house from the tornado.
2. What's the **cheapest** way to get to California by next week?
3. **Aren't** you going to the game today?
4. How many **people** live in your town?
5. Five feet is the **deepest** water I can go in, since I don't swim very well.
6. My dad has an uncanny **ability** to read my mind.
7. When he was running to catch the ball, he strained his right **triceps**.
8. Did the doctor have to use **forceps** when you were born?
9. His cell phone **beeped** in the middle of the speech.
10. Jack **heaped** pretzels into a bowl to share with John.

Day 92

```
G N I P E E H C S + F + + + Y
T + + + + + + W + + O + + + L
D P + + + + E + + + O + + + P
+ I E + + P + B + + T + + E A
+ + S W T + + A + + S + P + E
+ + + A + + + B + P T P + + H
D I S A B I L I T Y E + + S C
P + + + + L + E + R P O E + +
+ E + + + + I S I + S H P + +
+ + T P E R C N + + T + + L +
+ + + S + + G + G O + + + + E
+ + + + E + + + L + + + + + +
+ + + + + D + C + + + + + + +
+ + + + + + + I + + + + + + +
+ + + + + + + S + + + + + + +
```

(Over,Down,Direction)
ABILITY(4,7,E)
BABIES(8,4,S)
CHEAPLY(15,7,N)
CHEEPING(8,1,W)
CLOTHES(8,13,NE)
CREPT(7,10,W)
DISABILITY(1,7,E)

DISABLING(1,3,SE)
FOOTSTEPS(11,1,S)
PEOPLE(10,6,SE)
PEPPERING(15,3,SW)
SIDESTEP(8,15,NW)
SWEPT(9,1,SW)
WEPT(4,5,NW)

Day 99

```
D + + + R D + N D B R + I + +
+ E + + E E A + A E O + N + +
+ + L L + M G + O F L + H + B
+ + I I S D E A R O I + A A +
+ A + E A X E + L R A + L + +
B + L + H M + L I E S E E + +
+ A + A + + K + A + D + D + +
S + L R O L O C R P + + + + +
B E C A U S E C A + M + + + +
D + + + + + + + O L + I + + +
R A I L E D + + + + L B + + +
+ + + + + + + + + + + O + + +
+ + + + + + + + + + + + U + + +
+ + D E L I A R T + + + R + +
+ + + + + + + + + + + + + + +
```

(Over,Down,Direction)
BAILED(1,6,NE)
BALED(15,3,SW)
BECAUSE(1,9,E)
BEFORE(10,1,S)
BLACKMAILED(11,11,NW)
COLOR(8,8,W)
COLOUR(8,9,SE)
EXHALED(7,4,SW)

IMPALED(12,10,NW)
INHALED(13,1,S)
RAILED(1,11,E)
RAILROAD(9,8,N)
REGALED(5,1,SE)
SAILOR(11,6,N)
SALESMAN(1,8,NE)
TRAILED(9,14,W)

Day 97

Unscramble these:
1. kmaillbac   **blackmail**
2. ipmela   **impale**
3. lmae   **male**
4. fmeael   **female**
5. imal   **mail**
6. hali   **hail**
7. isla   **sail**
8. aels   **sale**
9. apli   **pail**
10. alpe   **pale**

Day 104

Unscramble these
1. gldpeola   **galloped**
2. levsyal   **valleys**
3. ynrai   **rainy**
4. ctsoleh   **clothes**
5. teteaatllt   **tattletale**
6. nslietma   **ailments**
7. gansiietrnr   **restraining**
8. hslware   **whalers**
9. nwaigil   **wailing**
10. eintratsrs   **restraints**

Day 107

Fill in the blank:

1. Mrs. Smith went to the police to voice her **complaint**.
2. After reading the note, Allison **wadded** it up and threw it away.
3. None of the **explanations** seemed to satisfy the crowd.
4. Why **can't** you fix the problem?
5. My dad and grandfather **planted** twenty acres of soybeans over the weekend.
6. Lisa **wanted** to go skiing, but tripped and broke her foot.
7. Did you see the news story about the prison **break**?
8. Jack and Matt helped look for a toddler who **wandered** away from the park.
9. Who **entertained** at the fair last summer?
10. My brother was **granted** leave to come home for the weekend from basic training.

Day 111

Unscramble these:

1. tednnteco   **contented**
2. ntpse   **spent**
3. evdnlteiat   **ventilated**
4. pnrenoetvi   **prevention**
5. sanonseic   **ascension**
6. dcenyce   **decency**
7. ewrhe   **where**
8. eddmneet   **demented**
9. eenrtr   **renter**
10. eltvnuae   **eventual**

Day 112

```
P S + B + + + + + + C N + + T
+ R N + E + + A + O E + + N +
+ + E O + F S + N E A + E + +
E + + V I C O T B + S S V + +
+ R + + E T E R + + S R E + +
+ W E N T N N + E I E E N + +
+ + T H T + T E D + N H T + +
+ + + M W + + A V + T T I + +
+ D E S C E N T T N + A L + +
+ N S T N U A + + I I F A + +
T + Y L L A U T N E V E T + +
+ + + + + + + N + + + E I + +
+ + + + + + + E + + + + O + +
+ + + + + + + P + + + + N + +
+ + + + + + + S + + + + + + +
```

(Over,Down,Direction)
ASCENT(8,2,SW)
ASSENT(11,3,S)
AUNTS(7,10,W)
BEEN(9,4,NE)
BEFORE(4,1,SE)
CONTENTMENT(11,1,SW)
DESCENT(2,9,E)
DISSENT(9,7,NE)

EVENTUALLY(12,11,W)
FATHERS(12,10,N)
INVENTIONS(11,10,NW)
PREVENTATIVE(1,1,SE)
SPENT(8,15,N)
VENTILATION(13,4,S)
WENT(2,6,E)
WHERE(5,8,NW)

Day 113

Fill in the blank:

1. On St. Patrick's Day, we'll **tint** the frosting **green**.
2. **Lean** the rake against the wall.
3. There was a **misprint** in the program. Janet was playing the part of the queen.
4. This antique is in **mint** condition.
5. **Between** having to **clean** my room and study for the final, I don't have any time to spare.
6. I think it's **mean** to leave him out.
7. Do you **screen** your calls with caller ID?
8. Give me a **hint** about your **Halloween** costume.
9. The doctor put a **splint** on my sprained finger.
10. My uncle had a **stint** in the Air Force.

Day 116

Unscramble these:

1. nmigiitspnr   **misprinting**
2. uqintnisg   **squinting**
3. secgeinnr   **screening**
4. rgnenieg   **greening**
5. oenturfe   **fourteen**
6. nstcnaee   **canteens**
7. engianm   **meaning**
8. rrnpstie   **printers**
9. wntrei   **winter**
10. eenregts   **greenest**

Day 118

Fill in the blank:

1. It **has been** very cold this winter.
2. We're going to plant green **beans** this spring.
3. Do you have any library **fines**?
4. **Moonshine** is homemade liquor.
5. Never getting enough sleep **undermined** Elizabeth's health.
6. My little sister **whines** when she doesn't get her way.
7. How many **spines** do **porcupines** have?
8. This handbook clearly **defines** the dress code.
9. The scent of the **pines** was really strong at the campsite.
10. Where are most of the coal **mines** in the United States?

Day 122

Unscramble these:

1. esusnhiot   **outshines**
2. scoebmni   **combines**
3. uelernnisd   **underlines**
4. ednsnri   **dinners**
5. sglhau   **laughs**
6. ebrka   **break**
7. afgrt   **graft**
8. nseeldic   **declines**
9. rtaef   **after**
10. htsfsa   **shafts**

Day 127

```
G + S + + + + F + N E + + + +
+ R + E + + A + O + A + + + +
+ + E + A T + I + + T + + + +
+ + A H T T B E R E F T D S
+ + + E T I E + + + N + + E W
+ + R + T E + D + + + N + N E
+ L + E + + S + + + + + E A
Y + P D + D E T A E P E R T
+ E + E + + D + H + + + + A I
R + + T + E + + + G + + H E N
+ + + F T + + + + U E + R G
T R E A T M E N T + A A + H +
+ + E R + + + + + R + + R T +
+ L + D + + + + T + + + D +
B + + + + + + + + + + + + +
```

(Over,Down,Direction)
BEREFT(8,4,E)
BLEATED(1,15,NE)
DRAFTED(4,14,N)
DRAUGHT(14,14,NW)
EATEN(11,1,S)
FATHERLY(8,1,SW)
GREATEST(1,1,SE)

HEART(13,10,SW)
REPEATED(13,8,W)
REPETITION(1,10,NE)
SEATED(3,1,SE)
SWEATING(15,4,S)
THREATENED(14,13,N)
TREATMENT(1,12,E)

Day 128

Form the contractions

1. you would or you had   <u>you'd</u>
2. he would or he had   <u>he'd</u>
3. she would or she had   <u>she'd</u>
4. we would or we had   <u>we'd</u>
5. I would or I had   <u>I'd</u>
6. who would or who had   <u>who'd</u>
7. why would   <u>why'd</u>
8. that would or that had   <u>that'd</u>

Day 130

Unscramble these:

1. lyltea   <u>lately</u>
2. eiairtsrg   <u>irrigates</u>
3. esgtar   <u>grates</u>
4. rtaesg   <u>greats</u>
5. enteisrats   <u>reinstates</u>
6. operbtsa   <u>probates</u>
7. eidancidt   <u>indicated</u>
8. ctalddesooni   <u>consolidated</u>
9. eaeddcut   <u>educated</u>
10. daolect   <u>located</u>

Day 131

Fill in the blank:

1. Jack <u>**dated**</u> Tim's sister in high school.
2. <u>**It's too bad**</u> we can't go swimming today.
3. She <u>**skated**</u> brilliantly in the Olympic Games.
4. <u>**Later**</u> this year, we're taking a trip to Belize.
5. That street is <u>**slated**</u> for repaving this summer.
6. I'm so <u>**grateful**</u> for your help.
7. His <u>**reinstatement**</u> will be effective on Monday.
8. She will be <u>**vacating**</u> the apartment next week.
9. Our company is <u>**consolidating**</u> several offices to save money.
10. My science teacher has been nominated for <u>**Educator**</u> of the Year.

Day 132

```
+ + + + + + + + + + + + + +
+ + D + + + + + + + S T A T E
+ S + E T A T S N I E R + + +
+ + K + D E + N + + + + G T +
R E L A T I O N S H I P R S +
N + T A T I C D + E A + A E +
+ O R A T I A A D + + T T T E
+ G I A C T N U T + + E A D +
+ + C T I O C G + I + F E U +
+ A + N A A L + + Y O + U R C
V + G + T B + + + L + N L G A
+ + + I + + O T S E T A L + T
+ + O + + + + R + T + + Y + E
+ N + + + + + P A + + + + +
L O C A T I O N + L + + + + +
```

(Over,Down,Direction)
DATING(8,6,SW)
DEDICATION(3,2,SE)
EDUCATE(15,7,S)
EDUCATION(10,6,SW)
GRATE(2,8,NE)
GRATEFULLY(13,4,S)
GREATEST(14,11,N)
HATE(10,5,SE)
LATELY(10,15,N)

LATEST(13,12,W)
LOCATE(7,10,NW)
LOCATION(1,15,E)
PROBATION(9,14,NW)
REINSTATE(12,3,W)
RELATIONSHIP(1,5,E)
SKATING(2,3,SE)
STATE(11,2,E)
VACATION(1,11,NE)

Day 135

Fill in the blank:
1. My little sister can be **timid** around strangers.
2. Sometimes, giving a speech can be **intimidating** for the speaker.
3. Why is everyone **congregating** at the window?
4. The police are **investigating** the robbery.
5. Since I don't speak Portugese, I'll need a **translator**.
6. He's not our **regular** mailman.
7. May I borrow your **calculator**?
8. The **criminal** left behind some **incriminating** evidence.
9. Susan was **nominated** for class president.
10. I sent Allison a letter **congratulating** her on her award.

Day 139

Unscramble these:
1. irginhbanet   **hibernating**
2. tinpitiganca   **anticipating**
3. esdtrpaae   **separated**
4. sstrmaeipa   **separatism**
5. olettanr   **tolerant**
6. eosotrrpa   **operators**
7. rgerasieroftr   **refrigerators**
8. ryroagmti   **migratory**
9. einndatgisrtgi   **disintegrating**
10. geiaopronct   **cooperating**

Day 142

Fill in the blank:
1. Jack **hesitated** before he dove off the board.
2. The bitter cold **penetrated** every layer of clothing I wore.
3. During the height of the flood, we **evacuated** to higher ground.
4. The wide belt **accentuated** her waist.
5. My eyes were **irritated** by the chlorine in the swimming pool.
6. His leg had to be **amputated**.
7. Mr. Jones **insinuated** that I hadn't done my best work on the project.
8. Who **illustrated** that book?
9. Alec **demonstrated** how to set up our tent.
10. John **graduated** from college last year and moved to New York City.

Day 147

Fill in the blank:
1. Who is your favorite **actor**?
2. I really don't want to **tote** that box up the hill.
3. What is the **total** value of this order?
4. I **wrote** a letter apologizing for **misquoting** him.
5. Lisa **voted** for him for Congress.
6. What was the strongest **motivating** factor in your decision to leave?
7. We need to meet **privately** to resolve the problem.
8. That's a really strange sound from the **motor**.
9. My aunt **doted** on her cats.
10. This picture doesn't completely **capture** the beauty of the mountains.

Day 151

Fill in the blank
1. Newspapers and magazines are part of the mass **media**.
2. For a treat, I bought my sister a **chocolate** bar.
3. **Aren't** you coming with us? Why not?
4. Kristin spoke very **candidly** about her experiences in New York.
5. Was that a **deliberate** attempt to confuse me?
6. In the winter, my grandparents like to go to a warmer **climate**.
7. A two-year-old can be very **obstinate**.
8. The jury is still **deliberating**.
9. The bat flew out of his hand, **breaking** the window.
10. We urged him to take **immediate** action.

Day 153

1. earg   **rage**
2. agfl   **flag**
3. agrd   **drag**
4. ngaege   **engage**
5. ugage   **gauge**
6. adgngiese   **disengage**
7. rtaeuog   **outrage**
8. gaigzz   **zigzag**
9. angs   **snag**
10. geamrap   **rampage**

Day 155

Fill in the blank
1. Look at these pictures. He's really **aged** since the first one was taken!
2. The unruly mob **rampaged** through the streets.
3. Kristin and Mark are **engaged**.
4. He **bragged** about his high score.
5. My mom **nagged** me until I cleaned my room.
6. We **flagged** down a tow truck to help us fix our flat tire.
7. Allison **zigzagged** down the ski run.
8. He was **outraged** at the price increase.
9. The play was **staged** outdoors.
10. Jack **lagged** behind the others because he was tired.

Day 156

```
D + + + + O + G + + G + + W +
+ I + + + U + + N E N + + A +
+ + S + + T + + N I I + + G +
+ + + E + R G G + A G + + G +
+ + + + N A A + + + G G + I +
+ + + + U G G N + + A I A N +
+ + G E E A N A + R + N G +
+ + I M + O + G I G B + + G G
+ N E + + U + + E G G + + N +
G N + + + S + + + M A I I + G
T + + + + L + + + + E G N + N
C R A G S Y + + + + A N N G I
+ F L A G G I N G P + + T E G
G N I G A P M A R + + + + + A
G N I G A T S + + + + + + + C
```

(Over,Down,Direction)

AGING(10,4,SE)
BRAGGING(11,8,N)
CAGING(15,15,N)
CRAGS(1,12,E)
DISENGAGEMENT(1,1,SE)
ENGAGEMENT(10,2,SW)
ENGAGING(14,13,NW)
FLAGGING(2,13,E)

GAGGING(14,7,NW)
GAUGING(7,4,SW)
NAGGING(8,6,SE)
OUTRAGEOUSLY(6,1,S)
PAGING(10,13,NE)
RAMPAGING(9,14,W)
STAGING(7,15,W)
WAGGING(14,1,S)

Day 159

1. elblde   **belled**
2. ltod   **told**
3. llewed   **welled**
4. eldoortf   **foretold**
5. esdelipmls **misspelled**
6. oltled   **tolled**
7. curllfela   **cellularf**
8. wdlesle   **swelled**
9. deqllue   **quelled**
10. lelomedw   **mellowed**

Day 163

1. The judge **polled** the jury after the verdict was heard.
2. My little sister really likes the **dollhouse** she got for her birthday.
3. Did you see the **seagull** swoop down and catch that fish?
4. The National Guard **patrolled** the streets after the hurricane.
5. After the election, the Democrats **controlled** the Senate.
6. She **mulled** over her choices.
7. The kitten **yelped** when I accidentally stepped on its tail.
8. We **pulled** the drapes shut.
9. Do you like that flavor of **lollipop**?
10. I like my ice cream sundae served with a **dollop** of whipped cream.

Day 165
Fill in the blank

1. I felt so **helpless** after I heard the news.
2. Lisa went to the **bank** before she left on her trip.
3. You were so **helpful**. How can I ever **thank** you?
4. Please leave me a **blank** check.
5. The chain made a loud **clank** against the metal door.
6. May I have a **drink** of water? I'm thirsty.
7. My uncle drove a **tank** in the Korean War.
8. My great grandfather learned how to start his car with a **crank**.
9. John broke his **ankle** skiing.
10. Please put your dirty dishes in the **sink** to be washed.

Day 167

1. llfuhytkna   **thankfully**
2. uleuhfnpl   **unhelpful**
3. nekbadl   **blanked**
4. nrkrpteas   **prankster**
5. nrenkfssa   **frankness**
6. udknr   **drunk**
7. usnk   **sunk**
8. kepsnda   **spanked**
9. taenrk   **tanker**
10. nkbidle   **blinked**

Day 169
Fill in the blank:

1. She tried to **wink** back her tears of frustration.
2. What do you **think** about our team's chances to win the championship this year?
3. We need one more **egg** to make the brownies.
4. Have you ever heard the bray of a **donkey**?
5. My dog can sit up and **beg** for a treat.
6. It was so hot, we ran through the **sprinkler** to cool off.
7. I like watching the lights of the city **twinkle** at dusk.
8. Do you like the color **pink**?
9. I tried to **slink** down in my chair so she wouldn't ask me to answer the question.
10. The tide tends to **ebb** and flow.

Day 170

1. slkisn   **slinks**
2. inwks   **winks**
3. nkstih   **thinks**
4. nzic   **zinc**
5. tlkswine   **twinkles**
6. symeonk   **monkeys**
7. ilernsksp   **sprinkles**
8. cobsweb   **cobwebs**
9. sggeg   **eggs**
10. issekrpnrl   **sprinklers**

Day 174

Unscramble these:

1. awbskayc   **swayback**
2. kdoeefcr   **foredeck**
3. ikaescs   **seasick**
4. ebnkcotlet   **bottleneck**
5. epcacok   **peacock**
6. oekrcdb   **bedrock**
7. neigbpssdr   **bedsprings**
8. gldrina   **darling**
9. gnuk   **gunk**
10. njsku   **junks**

Day 175

Fill in the blank.

1. Joe and Jim **bunked** together at camp this summer.
2. When we were driving in the mountains, I started to get **carsick**.
3. Brian had a **ringside** seat for the game.
4. Mr. Elliott, the science teacher, was **dunked** in the **dunk** tank at the fair.
5. Adam worked on a ranch this summer and learned about raising **livestock**.
6. The football bounced into the end zone for a **touch-back**.
7. The cat **slunked** off into the bushes with a bird in its mouth.
8. Jake cut a **hunk** out of the bread with his pocket knife.
9. Our company got some good **feedback** about the new product at the meeting.
10. What made you want to hang out with that **roughneck**?

Frequently Used Spelling Rules

FLOSS RULE

A one-syllable base word with one short vowel immediately before the final sounds of (f), (l), or (s) is spelled with ff, ll, or ss.

Examples:

off

ball

miss

Exceptions to this rule: yes, gas, bus, plus, this

RABBIT RULE

Double the consonants b, d, g, m, n and p after a short vowel in a two syllable word.

Examples:

rabbit

manner

dagger

banner

drummer

DOUBLING RULE

A base word ending in one consonant after an accented short vowel doubles the final consonant before a suffix beginning with a vowel.

Examples:

run + ing = running

stop + ed = stopped

hop+ ing = hopping

DROPPING RULE

A base word ending in silent "e" drops "e" before a suffix beginning with a vowel.

Examples.

hope + ing = hoping

shine + ing = shining

slope + ed = sloped

CHANGING RULE

A base word ending in "y" after a consonant changes "y" to "i" before any suffix (except one beginning with "i").

Examples:

baby + ies = babies

lady + ies = ladies

boy + s = boys

toy +s = toys

Remember: You change the babies not the boys!